TNTRIO MOVEMENT

BOOK - 6

Franklin Ysaac + Eliseo Rio Jr. + Gus Lagman

May 2023

Published in USA in May 2023 by
TATAY JOBO ELIZES,
Self-Publisher, under the permission and authorization of

Franklin Ysaac, et al
authors and copyright owners.

The copyright owner can withdraw this permission at his discretion without any objection from Tatay Jobo Elizes at any time. Printing of this book is using the present day method of Print-On-Demand (POD) system, where prints will never run out of copies to be available for posterity.
The copyright owner is free to republish with other publishers anytime.

KDP ISBN: 9798395160577
Independently Published

Disclaimer: Views are expressed by the author alone. Tatay Jobo Elizes does not knowingly publish false information and may not be held liable for the views of the author and right to free expression.

Contact: job_elizes@yahoo.com +
https://www.facebook.com/franklin.ysaac +
http://tinyurl.com/mj76ccq (amazon site) +
www.tatayjoboelizes.webs.com +
https://www.facebook.com/groups/399368500835109

Content

....

Preface

The main subject of this book and previous books is about results of the May 9, 2022 national elections in the Philippines.

A team of IT experts composed of the three(3) authors of these books have initiated moves to write about their findings and technical analyses of the election results.

The findings are well explained in many writings and postings in social media, particularly facebook, and the actions taken by them with the support of many sectors of society.

The updates had been recorded in previous books, published at amazondotcom, which are the following titles:

1–Truth Petition to Comelec (Initial book)
2—Truth Warriors-1
3—Initial Stages of Truth Petition
4—Truth Warriors-2
5—Truth Patriots-1
6—Writ of Mandamus Petition
7—TNTrio Movement Book-1
8—TNTrio Movement Book-2
9—TNTrio Movement Book-3
10- TNTRIO Movement Book-4
11–TNTRIO Movement Book-5
12—THTRIO Movement Book-6 (this one)

As this is a continuing movement, more books will be published from collection of writings and postings in the web to record all developments for posterity and guidance of all concerned.

....

1

On Leni Robredo – <u>TNTrio Movement</u> – <u>Mhel Mendez Bulabos</u> – by Franklin Ysaac – May 4, 2023

This expression of VP was very difficult as she couldn't afford to file election protest considering the staggering amount that would cost her.

At P500 per ballot of recount and the differential is insurmountable at 17 million votes, she couldn't raise the billions for a recount. The law says she has to raise her own money and not other people's money to pay for the recount.

Secondly, she was given the information by her lawyers and IT staff that the election was indisputably clean.

Third, she wasn't aware about #TNTrio's efforts from the early months. And nobody as in nobody ever believed what we were about to uncover about the fraudulent election results.

It was our desire and commitment not to solicit any support, financial or otherwise, from any political party as our campaign may be tainted and the regulatory body would dismiss outright our petition for being politically motivated.

We also wanted to spare the VP and other candidates from further bashing as they had enough of these trolls already.

Slowly, through our persistent efforts, we were able to unearth the rigging behind the election. Then we filed our TRO and mandamus before the Supreme Court to validate our claim that the election was fraudulent.

Despite our persistent requests for the transmission records, we have not received any positive response from the Comelec, the Telcos, and even the Supreme Court.

The cloud of doubt about the clean, honest and transparent election claimed by Comelec has began to emerge since we filed the petition last November 3, 2022.

For the record, while VP may have expressed her position that she may have lost the election, she never conceded as she believed the election was not clean, honest and transparent.

TNTrio is firmly convinced that the election was fraudulent given our indisputable presentation before the Supreme Court.

The Comelec and the Telcos must show proof of transmission that there were 21M votes counted during the first hour to prove that the election was clean, honest and transparent.

VP must already be aware of this petition and it's up to her to state her position with regard to our petition. The CBCP has voiced out already it's concern by coming out in a press statement supporting our petition.

- Franklin Ysaac

2
AN OPEN LETTER TO VP LENI ROBREDO – Roman Zarate – April 28, 2023

Being one of your very many supporters, please allow me to dare make an observation and suggestion to you.

1. Your silence in the wake of the Mandamus petition of the TNTrio has baffled and confused many of your supporters. They understood why you initially accepted the proclamation of Marcos and Sara. However, after your period of foreign speaking engagements and Angat Buhay projects, they now look to you for leadership and support in the efforts of the TNTrio and others to show that the election was rigged.

2. Please communicate with Gen Eliseo Rio and the TNTrio to understand what they are working hard to achieve against all odds and somehow show the people that you support their efforts to LEARN THE TRUTH. Your supporters and even the Liberal Party are now rudderless and many have lost heart for the fight for true justice and democracy in the Philippines.

Many are puzzled by your silence and have even wondered whether you are truly the leader we had all hoped for. Some have even spoken about giving up the fight and not voting in the next elections because it would be useless in the face of a biased COMELEC.

Where once hundreds of thousands and even millions rallied to your side, now not even 25 thousand have signed an online petition supporting the Mandamus petition.

Please come out once again and lead the people who are crying for justice and true democracy for our country. At this time, no other person exists who can do what ONLY YOU CAN. That is, to UNITE us once again. The country is crying out for your leadership.

PLEASE LEAD US NOW ...

Fred-Cyd Gallardo

Magpirma po tayo sa PEOPLE'S MANDAMUS:

https://chng.it/79gg9SqWmq

People's Mandamus to Compel Comelec to disclose True Transmission Logs. PLEASE SIGN AND SHARE THIS! You do not have to "CHIP IN".

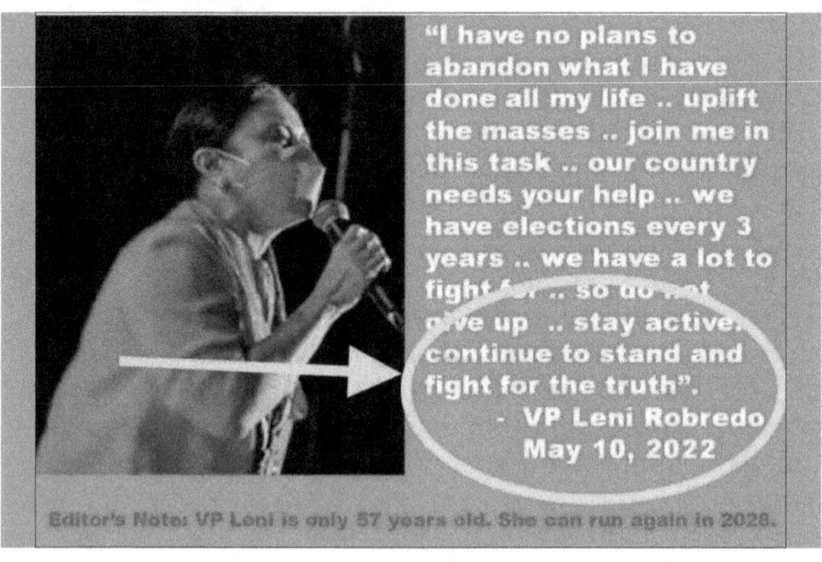

3
20,284 Signed the The Mandamus Petition as of May 5, 2023 – Hooray! – Posted by GP Tan III

PEOPLE'S MANDAMUS ONLINE PETITION To Compel Comelec to disclose True Transmission Logs

20,284 signers ! Marked @ 6.45 AM 5/5/2023 FRIDAY.

SHOUT OUT TO 15 millions +/- KAKAMPINKS, KINDLY JOIN and SIGN and SHARE !!!

....

4
Calling on all UP alumni and alumnae to join us in the May 9 rally – Franklin Ysaac – May 5, 2023

Calling on all UP alumni and alumnae to join us in the May 9 rally at the Comelec to protest the May 9 2022 election fraud.

Same with alumni and alumnae of the top 9 schools, DLSU, ADMU, UST …. And students from schools and universities all over the country .

Let's prove to ourselves that we are not only proud of our schools but we are also proud to be Filipinos who know how to fight for the truth and who know how to make our country free from human rights violations, political repression, ejk, foreign intervention, economic slavery, and illegitimate leaders.

Join us to show we love our country more than ourselves.

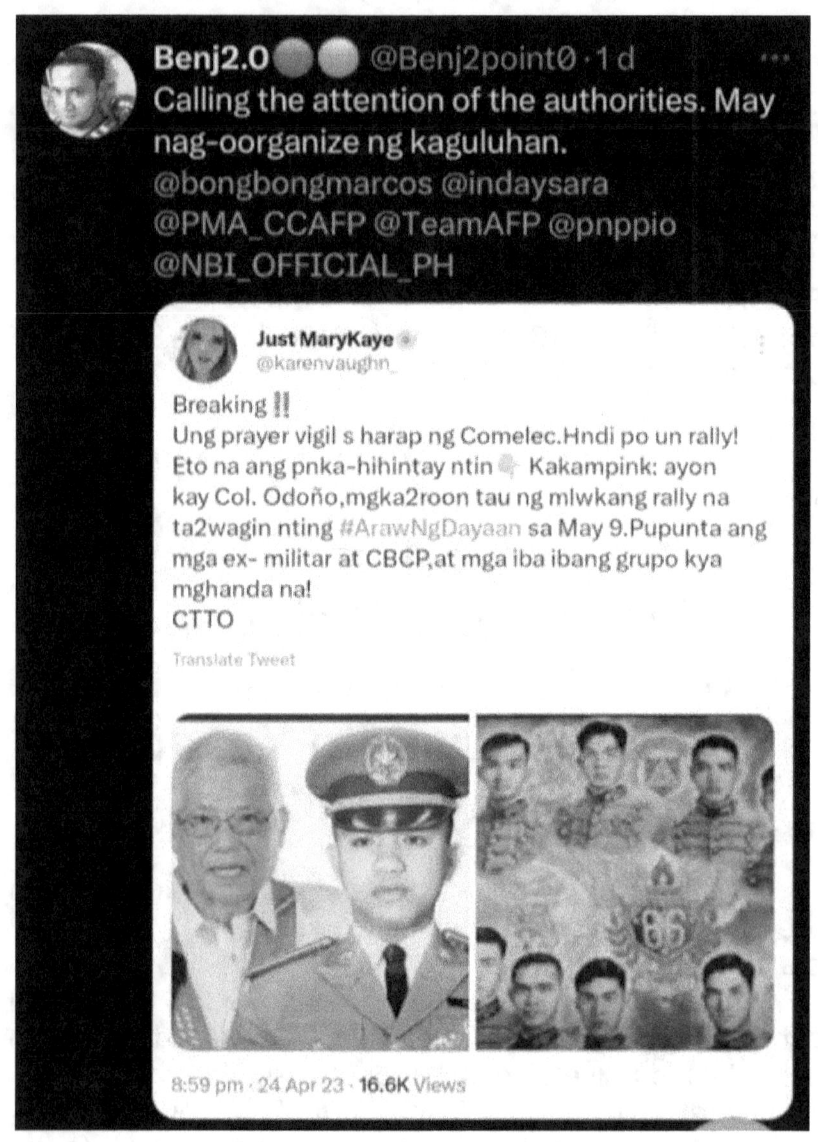

BB
@Z381969

Sa lahat ng patuloy na tumitindig para sa katotohanan, sana tumugon tayo sa panawagan ng TNTrio na makilahok sa pagtitipon sa Mayo 9 sa harap ng oficina ng COMELEC.

Hinihikayat at suportado tayo ng CBCP, UP Vanguards at koponan ng mga retiradong opisyal ng militar.

Translate Tweet

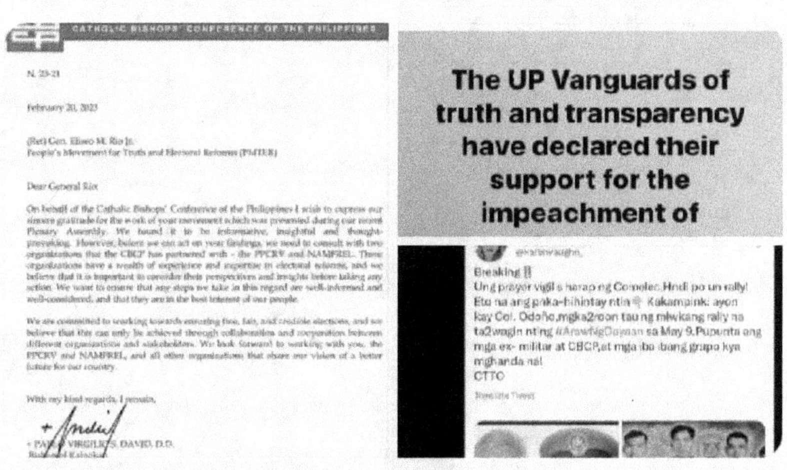

9:27 PM · 01 May 23 · **5,135** Views

5
TUMINDIG SA KATOTOHANAN
– Christine Astorga, Ph.D. –
May 5, 2023 – Translated by Dr. Ason Hipolito

https://m.facebook.com/story.php?story_fbid=6029642437089508&id=100001314354738&mibextid=Nif5oz

(copy and paste)

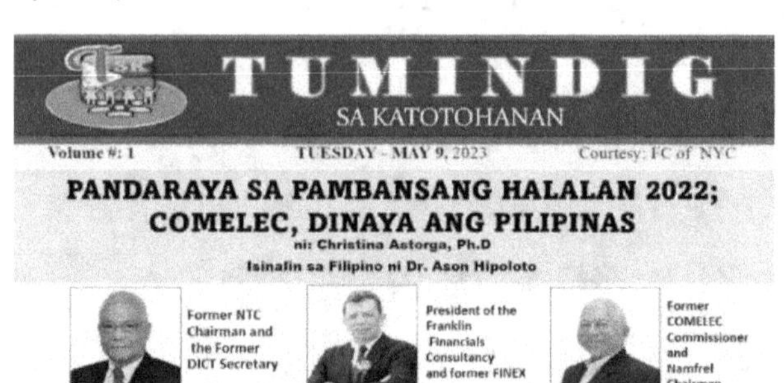

TUMINDIG
SA KATOTOHANAN

Volume #: 1   TUESDAY - MAY 9, 2023   Courtesy: FC of NYC

PANDARAYA SA PAMBANSANG HALALAN 2022; COMELEC, DINAYA ANG PILIPINAS

ni: Christina Astorga, Ph.D

Isinalin sa Filipino ni Dr. Ason Hipoloto

ELISEO RIO JR. — Former NTC Chairman and the Former DICT Secretary

FRANKLIN YSAAC — President of the Franklin Financials Consultancy and former FINEX

AUGUSTO C. LAGMAN — Former COMELEC Commissioner and Namfrel Chairman

Nang matapos ang Pambansang Halalan 2022 ng Pilipinas na si Ferdinand Marcos, Jr. at Sara Duterte ang nanalo ng may napakalaking lamang sa Opposition, at dineklara ni VP Leni ang kanyang pagkatalo dahil walang ebidensiya ng pandaraya, ayon sa kanyang mga abogado,nagdilim ang kapaligiran para sa lahat ng mga lumalaban para sa demokrasya. Animo'y iyon na ang katapusan ng daan, at ang panibagong yugto ng rehimeng Marcos, na may nakaambang Sara Duterte na hahalili pagkaraan ng anim (6) na taon, o marahil isa sa mga anak ni Marcos Jr., o isa sa mga kapatid ni Duterte ang susunod sa kanya.

Isang malagim na pangitain, hanggang may Tatlong Mago na dumating sa eksena, na sumusunod sa Tala ng Katotohanan, at ibinulgar ang pandaraya sa halalan. Sila ay binansagang **TNTrio** – ang acronym na TNT ay para sa **TRUTH and TRANSPARENCY,** at Trio para sa tatlong (3) Information Technology experts na naglantad sa pandarayang nagbigay daan sa nakamamanghang panalo ng Marcos-Duterte tandem. Sila ay armado ng mabibigat na credentials: Si **Retired BGen. Eliseo M. Rio Jr.** ay naging Chairman ng National Telecommunications Commission at Kalihim ng Department of Information and Communications Technology, at kasabayang nagsilbing Chairman ng COMELEC Advisory Council. Ilang taon din siyang nagsilbi bilang miyembro at Commander ng Technical Intelligence Group (MIG21) ng Intelligence Service of the Armed Forces of the Philippines (ISAFP). Si **Mr. Augusto C. Lagman** ay isa sa mga nagtayo ng Systems Technology Institute (STI) at naging Presidente ng Philippine Computer Society. Siya ay naging Commissioner ng COMELEC, at nakapagsilbi din bilang miyembro, Chairman at Presidente ng National Citizens' Movement for Free Elections (NAMFREL) ng halos apat na dekada. Si **Mr. Franklin F. Ysaac** ay ang Presidente ng Franklin Financials Consultancy Phils., Inc. at naging Presidente ng Financial Executive Institute of the Philippines (FINEX) noong 2004. Ang pagdaloy ng mga pangyayari ang naging dahilan na magtagpo ang mga hindi magkaka-kilalang tatlong mago sa isang panig ng digmaan para sa isang adhikain – ang katotohanan at integridad ng Pambansang Hal-

Ang TNTrio ay nagduda sa **20+ milyong boto** na ipinakita sa publiko ng Transparency Server nang 8:02pm, pagkatapos magsarado ang mga presinto ng 7:00pm. Ipinahayag ng COMELEC General Instructions (GI), Resolution 10762 noong Pebrero 16, 2022 na para sa halalan ng Mayo 09, 2022, pagkatapos isara ang botohan, kinakailangan munang maisagawa ang siyam (9) na pangunahing tungkulin ng Election Board bago mag-umpisa ng transmission ng Election Returns (ER). Ang oras na gugugulin para matapos ang 9 na tungkulin ay humigit-kumulang na labing-siyam (19) na minutos, na ang pinakamatagal gawin ay ang pag-imprenta ng walong kopya ng ER, ayon sa opisiyal na COMELEC Hands-On Lecture Demo Video of VCM (Vote Counting Machine) operations for the 2022 Elections, na salungat sa walong minuto na sinabi ng COMELEC na magugugol bago mag-umpisa ang VCM transmission. Maliwanag na sinasalungat ng COMELEC ang kanila mismong Demo Video. --

sundan p. 2

"Hybrid System ang Dapat Ipalit sa Fully Automated Election"

ni: Augusto Lagman

Hybrid na Sistema ng Eleksyon Nirekomenda noon ni dating NAMFREL Chairman Gus Lagman para sa Halalan 2022. Ang magbilang manually sa presinto, pagkatapos ay sabayan ng laptop. Itong laptop ang magtratransmit para sa canvassing, pagkatapos ay tuloy-tuloy na ang canvassing na automated. Ang bilangan sa presinto ay dapat manual para makita ng mga tao, dahil kung automated pati ang pagbibilang ay hindi natin alam kung tama ang pagbibilang. Kaya, mas mainam ang manual precint counting, tapos ay sundan ng automated canvassing.

"It's not the voting that's democracy, it's the counting ."-Tom Stoppard, British playwright, and screenwriter

1

TUMINDIG sa KATOTOHANAN

| Volume #: 1 | TUESDAY - MAY 9, 2023 | Courtesy: FC of NYC |

PANDARAYA SA PAMBANSANG HALALAN 2022

Makaraan pa lamang ng isang oras pagkasarado ng botohan ng 7:00pm, sinabi ni Ret. BGen. Rio Jr. (Sir Rio) na "ang kaduda-dudang 20+ milyong boto na nabilang na, at ito'y masasabing pinakamataas ng bilang ng boto na naitala sa unang oras sa buong kasaysayan ng halalan sa Pilipinas, kung hindi man sa buong mundo.

Sa unang oras, mula 7:00pm hanggang 8:00pm, ang pinakamaagang transmission ng ERs ay maaari lang mangyari ng bandang 7:19pm, kaya record-breaker ang 20+ milyong boto sa loob ng 41 minutos! Ito ay katulad rin ng nakakamanghang ikalawang oras, mula 8:00pm, ang mga botong nabilang ay bumagsak sa hindi maipaliwanag na 13.2+ milyong boto, gayong sa oras na ito, lahat ng tungkuling hinihingi ng General Instructions ay nairaos na sa unang oras".Habang may ilang milyon ang hindi pa nakakaboto, ang pagkaka-halal sa Presidente at Bise-Presidente, sa unang oras pa lamang, ay matuturing na fait accompli, dahil sa sumunod na apat (4) na araw ng bilangan, mayroon nakapagtatakang vote-ratio na hindi nag-iiba para sa lahat ng mga kandidato para sa Presidente at Bise-Presidente. Ayon kay Sir Rio na "ang gayong resulta ay nai-programa na, at kung sinuman ang nagmanipula sa resulta ng Transparency Server ay batid na ang "official results" ng halalan, bago pa man nagumpisa ang bilangan".

Ayon sa COMELEC, ang nakakamanghang bilis ng transmission ng Election Returns ay dahil matagumpay nilang naisa-ayos ang sistema para sa bilis. Kaya lang, hindi ang mabilis na VCM transmissions ang kinukuwestiyon ng TNTrio, dahil sa makabagong teknolohiya ay possible talaga iyon, kundi ang hindi kapani-paniwalang eksaktong oras na nag⬜umpisa ang mabilis natransmission, na 7:08pm, makatapos magsarado ng 7:00pm, dahil samatapos ang mga tungkuling hinihingi ng COMELEC bago mag-umpisa ang transmission. Ngunit nabanggit ang mas nakakagulat, kundi man nakakabahala, ay ang mga botong nabilang ng Transparency Server sa unang oras ay higit pa kaysa sa bilang na nata-transmit ng VCMs mula sa mga botohang presinto, gayong ang oras ng lahat ng mga proseso ay magkakasabay sa pinaka-maiksing segundo. COMELEC mismo ang nag⬜buko sa sarili nila nang ang kanilang Chairman ay nagpakita ng "Accumulated VCM Transmissions" graph sa publiko noong Oktubre 18, 2022, sa isang forum sa Ateneo de Manila University.   — sundan p. 3

UP Vanguard Statement

Eliseo Rio Jr.

A CALL FOR PEACEFUL PUBLIC PROTEST

We, the undersigned-UP Vanguards, signing in our individual capacity and our belief for Truth and Transparency, together with other individuals and organizations, call for peaceful, public protests in support of the impeachment of the Commissioners of the Commission on Elections and for the abolition of the Smartmatic partnership in future elections.

The COMELEC has failed the Filipino people and the Constitution by violating its mandate to protect the sanctity of the ballot by being the center of election irregularities and outright violations of the provisions of the Election Code.

1. It has allowed people with criminal records to run for public office, at many levels, forsaking its mandate to ensure that candidates with good moral character occupy elective Government offices.

- sundan p. 6

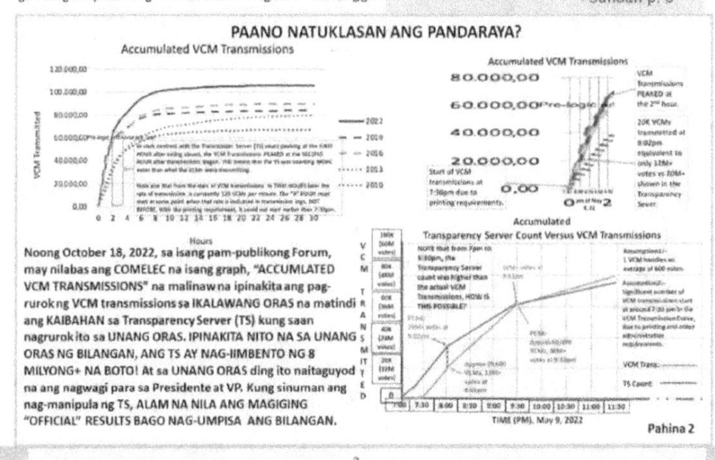

Noong October 18, 2022, sa isang pam-publikong Forum, may nilabas ang COMELEC na isang graph, "ACCUMLATED VCM TRANSMISSIONS" na malinaw na ipinakita ang pagrurok ng VCM transmissions sa IKALAWANG ORAS na matindi ang KAIBAHAN sa Transparency Server (TS) kung saan nagrurok ito sa UNANG ORAS. IPINAKITA NITO NA SA UNANG ORAS NG BILANGAN, ANG TS AY NAG-IIMBENTO NG 8 MILYONG+ NA BOTO! At sa UNANG ORAS ding ito naitaguyod na ang nagwagi para sa Presidente at VP. Kung sinuman ang nag-manipula ng TS, ALAM NA NILA ANG MAGIGING "OFFICIAL" RESULTS BAGO NAG-UMPISA ANG BILANGAN.

TUMINDIG sa KATOTOHANAN

Volume #: 1   TUESDAY - MAY 9, 2023   Courtesy: FC of NYC

PANDARAYA SA PAMBANSNG HALALAN 2022 NG PILIPINAS

Ni. Christina Astorga Ph. D/ Isinalin sa Filipino ni Dr. Ason Hipoloto

Pinakita ng COMELEC graph ng Okt.18 na ang VCM transmissions ay nag-rurok ng ikalawang oras mula nang mag-umpisa ang transmissions, at hindi tumutugma sa Transparency Server kung saan nagrurok sa unang oras sa kanilang Marso 23, 2023 graph, kung saan nang 8:02pm ang kadudang 20+ milyong boto ay nabilang ng Transparency Server, habang 12+ milyong boto lamang ang na-transmit ng mga VCMs sa parehong panahon. Ang Transparency Server ay nagbilang ng higit 8 milyong boto kaysa sa tinatransmit ng VCMs at ito ay walang alinlangang pandaraya. Ang Transparency Server ay nag-imbento ng mga boto sa unang oras ng bilangan para lang maitatag ang kamangha-manghang panalo nina Marcos at Duterte. Kung ang Parish Pastoral Council for Responsible Voting (PPCRV) at ang NAMFREL-LENTE Random Manual Audit (RMA), sa kanilang "parallel count" ay naipagtibay ang COMELEC count, iyon ay sa kadahilanang ang mga binilang nila ay nakabatay sa parehong inimbentong datos. Sila ay mga di-sadyang kasabwat sa pandaraya ng COMELEC.

Nagkasa ng **dalawang hamon ang TNTrio sa COMELEC.** Una, *ipakita ng COMELEC sa publiko kung paano matatapos lahat ng hinihinging tungkulin sa loob ng 8 minutos laban sa 19 minutos, bago mag-umpisang mag-transmit ang mga VCMs.* Ikalawa, *ilabas ng COMELEC ang transparency data na siyang batayan ng "Accumulated VCM Transmissions" graph na kanilang ipinakita sa publiko, kung saan nagrurok ng 20+ milyong boto ang Transparency Server sa unang oras, habang ang VCM count ay 12+ milyong boto lang ang na-transmit sa parehong unang oras.* Nabigo ang COMELEC na harapin ang 2 paghamon. Makaraan ang anim na buwang paghihintay para ilabas ng COMELEC ang transmission logs, dumulog ang TNTrio sa Korte Suprema para sa isang Petition for Mandamus upang utusan ang COMELEC na tumupad sa kanilang obligasyon ayon sa Constitution na maging tapat at makatotohanan. *Binigyan ng Korte Suprema ang COMELEC ng sampung (10) araw upang tumugon sa Mandamus, ngunit bigo pa rin sila.* Kung ang COMELEC ay hawak ang transmission logs ng 20+Milyong boto, hindi ba madaling ipakita kaagad ang mga iyon?

Tila wala silang transmission logs dahil ang ibinigay nila noong Marso 23, 2023 kay Ret. Col. Odoño, na nagbantang maghahain ng Impeachment Case laban sa limang (5) COMELEC Commissioners, at kay Sir Rio, ay hindi **Sa public online Forum noong Abril 15 na "Ano Ang Kabuluhan ng Pandaraya sa Election at ng Mandamus Case sa Buhay Mo?,"** iprinisenta ni Sir Rio ang DIREKTANG EBIDENSIYA ng pandaraya, lagpas pa sa kasaganaan ng circumstantial evidence, gamit ang mga kinatawang datos na COMELEC mismo ang naglabas sa kanilang website, at mapanlinlang na sinabing transmission logs ang mga reception logs. Naipakita ni Sir Rio kung paano natanggap ng Transparency Server ang ER sa ganitong oras bago pa man naitransmit ng

VCM ang datos mula sa presinto. transmission logs kundi mas lalo nitong nasira ang kredibilidad ng COMELEC at pinalala ang lumalaking paghihinala na sistematikong dinaya nila ang bansa. Mayroon ba talagang hawak na transmission logs ang COMELEC para sa 20+milyong boto?

May isang insidente na natanggap ng Transparency Server ang ER dalawang (2) oras bago pa man natransmit ng VCM ang ER. Paanong masasabi na may natanggap ang Transparency Server ng datos na hindi pa nata-transmit, puwera na lang kung ito ay kargado na ng mga boto bago pa man nagbotohan.Sa isang vlog ni Maharlika, isang dating matalik na kaibigan ni Lisa Marcos at insider sa Marcos circle, ngunit naging whistle-blower, kinumpirma niya ang mga napansing pandaraya ng TNTrio ukol sa Halalan 2022. Sa video-clip na pinapainig ang usapan ng dalawa nung Mayo 08, isang araw bago ng halalan, alam na ni Lisa kung ano ang magiging resulta ng halalan. Para makabawi sa ikinagalit ni Maharlika tungkol sa kanyang ticket sa Miting de Avance, inimbitahan siya ni Lisa na pumunta ng Mayo 09 sa ganap na 7:00pm sa isang lihim na lugar para mapanood niya ang isang "secret counting session like a PPCRV", para makagawa siya ng scoop sa pagkakapanalo ni BBM, ngunit bandang 9:00pm na lang niya ipapakita sa kanyang online vlog

Ito ang nagbabagang tanong ni Sir Rio: "Bakit isang araw bago ng halalan ay siguradong-sigurado si Lisa na mananalo si BBM pagtuntong ng 9:00pm ng Mayo 09? Bakit siya siguradong-sigurado at ginawa pang piling handog ang session na iyon paramakabawi kay Maharlika? Paano niya nahulaan na sa unang 2 oras ng bilangan, ang Transparency Server results na napapanood ng publiko ay aayon para sa kanyang mister? Madame Lisa, ito ba ang ginawa mo nang summer ng 2022?". Ang sagot sa mga katanungang ito ay ang pahayag ng TNTrio na "ang resulta ng Transparency Server ay malayong mangyari, kundi man imposible, ayon sa siyensiya ng Statistics, Mathematics at Logic. Kung sinuman ang nagmanipula ng Transparency Server results ay alam na niya ang "official results" ng halalan bago pa man nag-umpisa ang bilangan.Niloko ng COMELEC ang bansa at ang bansa ay nadaya. Ang dating Australian Senator Lee Rhiannon, Commissioner ng International Observer Mission ay nagpahayag tungkol sa Halalan 2022 na "Ang ebidensiya ay katakut-takot....Marcos Jr. at Sara Duterte ay hindi nahalal ng lehitimong paraan."-

karugtong buhat pp.1-2

Ang Pag mamahal sa bayan ay hindi nagtatapos sa eleksyon at sa mga kandidato ng sinuportahan natin.

TUMINDIG sa KATOTOHANAN

Volume #: 1   TUESDAY - MAY 9, 2023   Courtesy: FC of NYC

BREAKING NEWS!

RET. COL. LEONARDO O. ODONO, PMA Class of 1964 will be filing articles of impeachment in Congress against the five Commissioners of Comelec for the violation of the Constitution.

"Comrades and friends, The truth seekers', our search for the truth about those 20M votes supposed to have been counted at precinct level and transmitted to the transparency server of Comelec within only one hour after close of the 2022 election, is done.

Comelec refused to release proof of transmission of the questionable 20M votes which I requested in a letter I sent to the poll body, on November 26, 2022 - in the exercise of my constitutional right of access to information of public concern in the hands of a government agency, within the purview of the Freedom of Information regime in the country. It is the same material information jointly requested, earlier than I did, by Gen. Eli Rio, Mr. Augusto Lagman and Mr. Frank Ysaac, the TnTrio.

The refusal of Comelec to release my requested information in 15 days as required by law, and credible evidence our Movement has obtained in our four-month search, indicate that there was no such transmission of 20M votes, and those 20M votes were in fact non-existent. That election was rigged!

Given such troubling circumstances, I have decided, as a concerned citizen, I must file *Articles of Impeachment in Congress* against the five Commissioners for culpable violation of the Constitution. On March 10, 2023, I sent a final notice, attached, giving Comelec seven days to provide me and the public, that proof of transmission of the supposed 20M votes, failing in which will constrain me to file Articles of Impeachment in Congress against the five commissioners.

Another election is coming in 2025. Regardless of the outcome of the impeachment case, I will file in ten days, or soon after a congressperson makes an indorsement of the Articles of Impeachment required by law, it is my intention, and my hope, that my action will spur a serious effort on the part of our decision-makers to stop this vicious cycle of every election being tainted by irregularity.

I need your support in this difficult endeavor. I feel, I must pursue to the conclusion. I will appreciate your sharing this email with as many friends as you can reach.

Thank you.

Col. Leonardo O. Odono (Ret.)

Paranaque City
March 24, 2023
Atty. George Erwin M. Garcia
Chairman, Commission on Elections
Intramuros, Manila

SUBJECT: **PAMPUBLIKONG PAGTATALO - ARAW NG DAYAAN SA COMELEC**

Ginoong COMELEC Chairman,

Naisip ko na ang Mayo 9, 2023 ay ang unang anibersaryo ng Araw ng Dayaan sa Comelec. Maaaring gusto mong gawing banal na araw para sa inyong organisasyon, Sir, sa pamamagitan ng pagsagot sa mga tanong at isyu na aking binanggit sa aking liham noong March 29, 2023, sa isang pampublikong pagtatalo kung saan sina General Rio at ako ay magtutunggali sa inyo, Sir, at sa anim na iba pang Komisyoner. Maaari mo ring isama, Sir, ang iyong mga blogger, na sabi nila ay mula sa Namfrel, bilang mga resource persons - sila na patuloy na nangangakong walang anumang mga kahina-hinalang aktibidad sa nakaraang eleksyon - gayong ang Namfrel mismo ay nagpahayag na may mga flaw sa software ng eleksyon sa kanilang opisyal na ulat sa Comelec at nagbabala ng posibleng dayaan.

Sana, Sir, matapos ang 59 na araw ng pag-aalinlangan at pag-iisip mula nang aking liham noong March 29, 2023, makakatugon ka nang tapat sa aking mga katanungan sa ating debate.

Bakit mo ibinigay sa akin at kay General Rio ang Reception Logs - o tawagin natin itong Deception Logs - sa halip na ang patunay ng pagpapasa ng 20m votes, ang Transmission Logs mula sa precinct level hanggang sa Transparency Server ng Comelec na nagpapakalat ng bahagyang at di-opisyal na resulta. Hindi mo ba kami nilinlang, pati na rin ang publiko, Sir, sa pagsasabing ibibigay mo na sa amin ang Transmission Logs. Kung gayon, bakit po, Sir? Dahil po ba wala talaga yung 20 million votes? Gusto ko lang malaman kung saan galing yun?

Ang opisyal na Comelec accumulated VCM report graph na inilabas mismo ng Comelec sa isang pampublikong forum ukol sa eleksyon ng Ateneo University noong October 18, 2023, ay nagpapakita ng mga accumulated votes na umabot ng 12 milyon sa isang oras matapos ang eleksyon noong Mayo 9, 2023. Gayunman, ang Deception Logs na ibinigay sa akin at kay General Rio noong March 23, 2023, ay nagpakita ng mga accumulated votes na umabot ng 20m+ votes. Parehong Comelec report sa accumulated votes sa parehong oras pero iba-iba ang accumulated votes na nakapaloob sa mga ito?

Saan po ninyo nakuha ang dagdag na 8m na boto? Hindi ba't pre-loaded ang mga boto na iniulat bilang hindi opisyal at bahagyang ulat mula sa hindi opisyal na server ng Comelec? Maaaring ito ay nangyari dahil sa "software flaws" tulad ng ibinunyag ng Namfrel, o kaya naman ay "typo errors" na gusto ipakalat ng Comelec? At bakit nilaktawan ng Comelec ang babala ng Namfrel tungkol sa posibleng pandaraya?

Ano po ang dahilan kung bakit kinailangan ng Comelec ang 252 araw mula nang unang humingi ng ebidensiya ng pagpapadala ng 20m na boto ang TNT Trio, bago sila sumagot sa amin? Ganun na po ba kahirap at katagal mag-doktor ng mga ulat sa pagpapadala? Hindi po ba nilabag ng Comelec ang aming karapatan sa konstitusyon sa paglaktaw ng 15-araw na deadline na kinakailangan ng batas upang magbigay ng impormasyon katulad ng sa amin?

Ang aking huling tanong, Sir, meron po ba talaga 20m na boto?

Ginoong Chairman, ang pagtatalo sa publiko, na isasahimpapawid sa mga Pilipino nang live o replay, ay magpapaliwanag kung napunta sa mga kandidato na kanilang binoto ang kanilang mga boto, o kung naglaro lamang ng malupit ang SmartMagic at ang mga katuwang nito. At the same time, magbibigay ito sa inyo ng pagkakataon upang ipaliwanag ang inyong panig sa bawat isyu.

Tunay na sumasaiyo,
Col. Leonardo O. Odoño (Ret.)

TUMINDIG sa KATOTOHANAN

Volume #: 1   TUESDAY - MAY 9, 2023   Courtesy: FC of NYC

FRANKLIN YSAAC

Let me cut this whole matter of fraudulent results into this scenario which I described last year and which was validated by the expose of my colleague Eli Rio:

1. Smartmatic provided the automated election system which is a seamless process or straight through processing from casting of ballot, to counting , to printing of election returns and transmission reports.

2. The automated election system was witnessed by independent IT and was presumed to be perfect .

3. During the actual automated election process, the system was cut into parts which overrode the approved automated system.

4. The ERs were produced and the transmission reports were made.

5. The ERs and Transmission reports were given to political parties and PPCRV. The political parties kept the ERs but did not keep the transmission reports. These transmission reports eventually faded as the papers used were thermal paper.

6. We asked for copies of these transmission reports but we were ignored.

7. The ERs were eventually transmitted via telcos and were recorded under call detail reports.

8. We filed mandamus before SC to preserve the election data . Response was moot because they published the transmission logs.

9. We filed supplemental petition because the published transmission logs were not true and they were merely reception logs.

10. The whole process which was supposed to be seamless or straight through never happened. The ERs time logs do not reflect the same time logs even in reception logs. The ERs were transmitted much much later than the published reception logs giving rise to falsification of data.

11. The time logs from VCMs via Telco to Transparency server are supposed to be synchronized.

12. But what happened to the election data which passed through telcos but didn't end up in the transmission servers?

My judgment as IT is where is the real server or transparency server ?

In my Fb post last year, I mentioned that there is a strong possibility there are at least two transparency servers. One which is pre loaded and another which is the true transparency server ?

Questions:

A. Where are these data which were supposed to be transmitted by telco to the real server?

B. Who ordered the changes

In the automated system which is apparently not a seamless or straight through processing system ?

C. It the changes showed the apparent and perhaps deliberate attempt to change the results of the election, then those officials responsible have committed a serious crime?

WHY SIGNING THE PEOPLE'S MANDAMUS PETITION IS IMPORTANT!

Type: https://chng.it/79gg9SqWmq

The government's power comes from the people, who express their will through fair and honest elections. However, there is evidence of election cheating during the May 9, 2022 Philippine national elections.

The organization is responsible for making sure elections are fair; COMELEC, has not done a good job on explaining the anomalous vote-count results. Instead of giving the public the real transmission logs, which show the real vote count, they gave an unverified report of data that the transparency servers got. This report was passed off as transmission logs, but it was really just 'reception logs.'

It is important for all elections to be fair and honest for a healthy democracy. Filipinos have a constitutionally guaranteed right to information on matters of public concern and to demand proof that their votes were counted properly. They also have the right to demand that COMELEC address the allegations of election cheating in a prompt and truthful manner.

A government that is run by individuals perceived as illegitimate, lack public support will not be able to effectively serve the people.

It is extremely important for Filipinos to know the truth of whether the May 9 elections was in fact rigged, and if so, for the legitimately elected candidates to be proclaimed.

TUMINDIG sa KATOTOHANAN

Volume #: 1   **TUESDAY - MAY 9, 2023**   Courtesy: FC of NYC

PEOPLE'S MOVEMENT
FOR TRUTH, JUSTICE AND REFORMS

Ang PEOPLE'S MOVEMENT FOR TRUTH, JUSTICE AND RE-FORMS (PMTJR) ay koalisyon ng iba't ibang samahan at indibidwal na nag tataguyod ng Katotohanan, Katarungan at Repormang Panlipunan. Ang mga FOUNDING Convenor nito ay sina Ret. General Eliseo Rio ng UP VAN-GUARD, Atty Ricky Tomotorgo ng Bun-yog Pagkakaisa Party, Boni Macaranas ng People's Choice Movement, Waldy Carbonelll ng Kawal ng Demokrasya at Ago Pedalizo ng Filipino -American Human Rights Alliance. Kasama rin sina Atty Luke Espiritu, Engr Berteni "Toto" Causing , Rudy Roxas at si Ret. Col Leonardo Odoño. Patuloy na LUMALA-WAK ang People's Movement for Truth, Justice and Reforms. Ito ay bukas sa lahat ng Pilipinong naniniwala sa PRIN-SIPYO ng Katotohanan, Katarungan at Repormang Panlipunan.

The International Observer's Mission (IOM), whose members are composed of over 60 people from 11 countries, ran for five months and monitored the campaign period, election day, and post-election period until June 22. It reported that " This election does not meet the standard of " free and fair" because of those prevailing condition that robbed the voters of access to reliable information, access to the voting places without intimidation and a credible vote counting system. This election cannot be declared 'free and fair" until all the illegal acts that have marred the process are dealt with. - May 19, 2022

UP Vanguard Statement

Ni: ELISIO RIO, JR.   Mula sa p. 2

2. It surreptitiously printed tens of millions of ballots without independent supervision and observers in violation of procedures.

3. It changed the source codes of the voting machines and the allied electronic equipment without any supervision and without informing the independent observers.

4. It configured and inserted the SD cards that run the Vote Counting Machines (VCMs) without supervision and without foreknowledge of independent observers as to the programs and algorithms that went into the SD cards.

5. It conducted a fraudulent count of the votes using the combination of the altered source codes and the insertion of the unaudited SD cards. As a result of the confluence of the above factors, and without thinking that knowledgeable and competent information technology professionals were watching every bit of information that was released by COMELEC, anomalous and highly irregular and improbable results were released to the public. In one instance, data released by none other than the COMELEC Chairman himself, contradicted the results from the reception logs that were provided by COMELEC.

Perhaps with the foreknowledge that the justice system would eventually acquit them, they violated with impunity a Supreme Court order to provide the Transmission Logs within a Court prescribed deadline. They still have not formally complied with the order to submit the Logs as of today. We cannot allow a crooked COMELEC, NOW OR EVER, be the dictator of who will govern us, through their insidious machinations or through the Smartmatic machines banned even in its own country of origin. That is up to the Filipino voter who once trusted them to count our votes honestly and accurately.

ISULONG ANG LABAN PARA SA KATOTOHANAN, KATARUNGAN AT REPORMANG PANLIPUNAN!
-PMTJR
PEOPLE'S MOVEMENT FOR TRUTH, JUSTICE AND REFORMS

Franklin Ysaac posted the following: (May 5, 2023)

The previous articles or images are summaries of our efforts Re May 9 2022 pandaraya.

Be witness on May 9 2023 and join rally at the Comelec to protest pandaraya .

....

6
Final Tally: Leni Robredo – 14,822,051 vs BBMarcos – 11.104,175 (study facts below) – May 5, 2023

SO: VP Leni Robredo's "14,822,051 against BBMarcos 11,104,175. ✳ SINO ngayon ang "totoong nanalo at dapat nasa Malacanang, SINO ?. Santos Aljo: TS NOW HISTORY: P BB Marcos Jr's father ex-P FE Marcos was "proven to have 'cheated beyond reasonable doubt "during the HALALAN 86': Thus, "ousted or kicked out of "his BOGUS PRESIDENCY during the 4 days protest from Feb.22 to 25 at the EDSA People Power Revolution. Presumed that the *10,807,197 votes of Marcos was "manipulated by Marcos COMELEC "against the *9,291,716 of P Cory Aquino (RIP). EVENTUALLY: Corazon "Cory" Cojuangco Aquino (RIP) was "installed & took her oath as the 'legitimate 11th President of the Republic of the Philippines at Club Filipino.¶

HISTORY REPEATED? If 20 Million votes, "proven beyond reasonable doubt had been "manipulated by ex-PRRD30's COMELEC, & added to Unity party candidate BB Marcos Jr. for president; giving a "total of 31,104,175: *Deduct 20 million manipulated or questionable votes, the 'legitimate votes of BBM should only be 11,104,175: TAMA BA? SEE 1st photo below. ¶

PIO DURAN JALBAY TAMBAYAN
Santos Aljo · 1h · 🌐

"Hindi lang mga gintong nakatago sa maraming banko sa labas ng bansa, ang minama (inherited) nina Bongbong sa amang Marcos kundi ang kasamaan din: itong DAYAAN SA HALALAN! "
Ang susunod nito ay > NAKAWAN KALIWAT KANAN SA PONDO NG PAMAHALAAN! GUMISING NA KAYO KABABAYAN! Sumali sa pagtipon tipon!

....

7
COMMON SENSE AND SIMPLE LOGIC – Eliseo Rio Jr – May 5, 2023

There is just one simple test to show, without any doubt, whether the 2022 Election was RIGGED OR NOT. It is based on COMMON SENSE AND SIMPLE LOGIC. If it fails this test, ALL other tests, no matter how accurate they may seem to be were just part of AN elaborate RIGGING Process.

That test is simply this. In a clean and honest election the number of Election Returns (Ers) being TRANSMITTED by the VCMs must always match the Ers being RECEIVED by the Transparency Server at any time. IT IS NOT POSSIBLE FOR THE TS TO RECEIVE MORE Ers THAN WHAT ARE BEING TRANSMITTED BY THE VCMs AT ANYTIME! That is why it is important for COMELEC to show to the public BOTH the Reception Logs (which it already did upload in its website last March 23) and the Transmission Logs verified with the Telcos' Call Data Records (CDR). COMELEC up to now REFUSE to show the latter. But unknowingly, COMELEC did show an "Accumulated VCM Transmissions" in a Forum held last October 18, 2022, that depicted that VCM transmissions PEAKED at the SECOND HOUR. This was even proudly confirmed by the COMELEC Spokesperson himself!

Superimposing the graph plotted from the Reception Logs uploaded last March 23 in the COMELEC website, which PEAKED at the FIRST HOUR, it will be clearly seen that in the first TWO HOURS after voting closed ay 7pm of May 9, 2022, that the Transparency Server was receiving more Ers than what the VCMs were transmitting. And in that two hours "tapos na ang boksing" for the Presidency and VP positions.

Whoever manipulated the TS results already knew who the winners were even before the counting started.

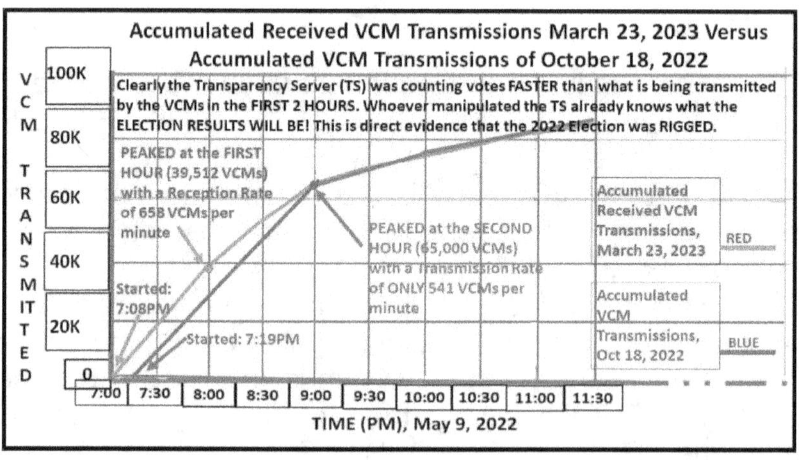

....

8
MORE THAN ENOUGH TIME –
Franklin Ysaac – May 5, 2023

Thus far, we gave respondents more than enough time to comment on a mandamus which is long overdue

. Except for Comelec, JCO where Solgen conveniently sought extension and Jco haven't convened yet respectively, these are not acceptable responses and we shall make the necessary responses . With regard to telco and XXXinyoXXXatic who haven't replied yet, this puts them in a situation where they are waiving their rights and we shall seek our own manifestation and motion so SC can take cognizance of the no responses.

Delays and more delays on simple mandamus case are part of respondents convenient excuses to hide the truth .

Judge their actions for yourselves.

People have the constitutional right to know which is the premise of our mandamus case.

This puts SC in a position to make final decision or suggest oral arguments or just submit respective memoranda.

We are upbeat on this case and we represent the millions of Filipino voters who have deprived of their right to know under freedom of information act.

Let's see how this unfolds in the coming days.

....

9

DELERELICTION OF DUTY BY SOLGEN – Franklin Ysaac – May 6, 2023

More excuses from respondents!

Read this letter response from Solgen re CAC and JCOCAE delayed response . " Hindi pa sila nag convene despite the rule they should meet as early as six months after Election Day!

Figure out what they are doing ? Isn't this dereliction of duty ?

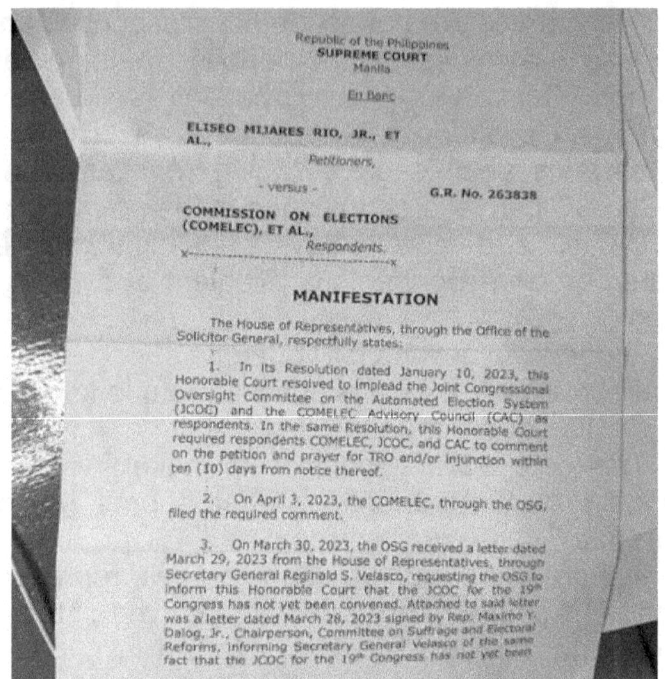

Republic of the Philippines
SUPREME COURT
Manila

En Banc

ELISEO MIJARES RIO, JR., ET AL.,

   Petitioners,

  - versus -   G.R. No. 263838

COMMISSION ON ELECTIONS (COMELEC), ET AL.,

     Respondents.

x- -x

MANIFESTATION

The House of Representatives, through the Office of the Solicitor General, respectfully states:

1. In its Resolution dated January 10, 2023, this Honorable Court resolved to implead the Joint Congressional Oversight Committee on the Automated Election System (JCOC) and the COMELEC Advisory Council (CAC) as respondents. In the same Resolution, this Honorable Court required respondents COMELEC, JCOC, and CAC to comment on the petition and prayer for TRO and/or injunction within ten (10) days from notice thereof.

2. On April 3, 2023, the COMELEC, through the OSG, filed the required comment.

3. On March 30, 2023, the OSG received a letter dated March 29, 2023 from the House of Representatives, through Secretary General Reginald S. Velasco, requesting the OSG to inform this Honorable Court that the JCOC for the 19th Congress has not yet been convened. Attached to said letter was a letter dated March 28, 2023 signed by Rep. Maximo Y. Dalog, Jr., Chairperson, Committee on Suffrage and Electoral Reforms, informing Secretary General Velasco of the same fact that the JCOC for the 19th Congress has not yet been

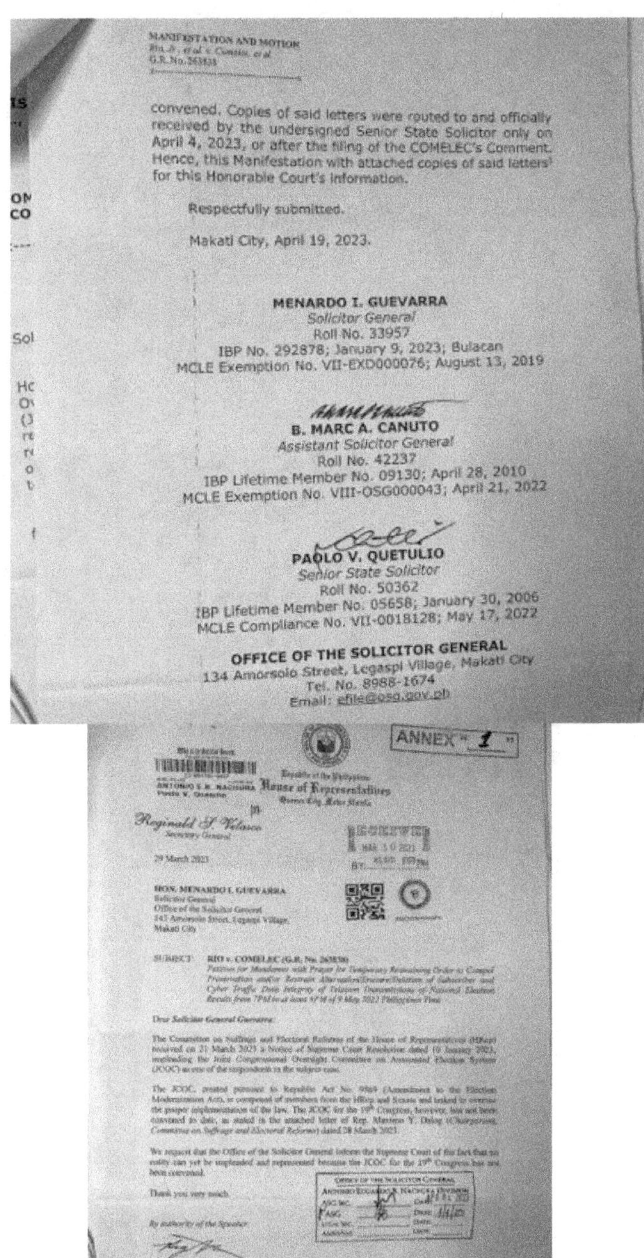

MANIFESTATION AND MOTION
Rio, Jr., et al. v. Comelec, et al.
G.R. No. 263533

convened. Copies of said letters were routed to and officially received by the undersigned Senior State Solicitor only on April 4, 2023, or after the filing of the COMELEC's Comment. Hence, this Manifestation with attached copies of said letters[1] for this Honorable Court's information.

Respectfully submitted.

Makati City, April 19, 2023.

MENARDO I. GUEVARRA
Solicitor General
Roll No. 33957
IBP No. 292878; January 9, 2023; Bulacan
MCLE Exemption No. VII-EXD000076; August 13, 2019

B. MARC A. CANUTO
Assistant Solicitor General
Roll No. 42237
IBP Lifetime Member No. 09130; April 28, 2010
MCLE Exemption No. VIII-OSG000043; April 21, 2022

PAOLO V. QUETULIO
Senior State Solicitor
Roll No. 50362
IBP Lifetime Member No. 05658; January 30, 2006
MCLE Compliance No. VII-0018128; May 17, 2022

OFFICE OF THE SOLICITOR GENERAL
134 Amorsolo Street, Legaspi Village, Makati City
Tel. No. 8988-1674
Email: efile@osg.gov.ph

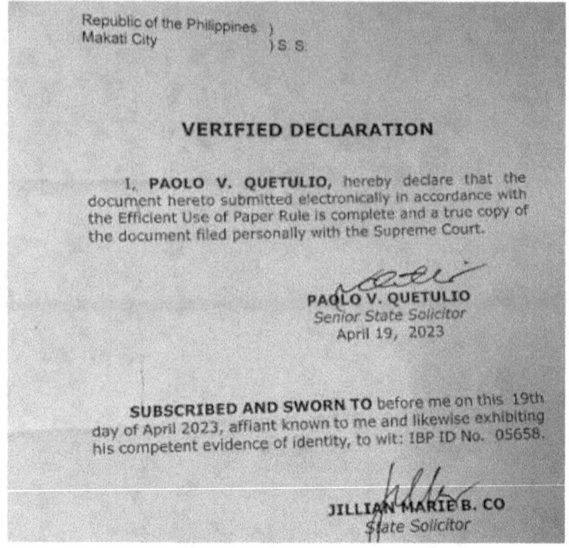

Republic of the Philippines)
Makati City   ) S. S.

VERIFIED DECLARATION

I, **PAOLO V. QUETULIO,** hereby declare that the document hereto submitted electronically in accordance with the Efficient Use of Paper Rule is complete and a true copy of the document filed personally with the Supreme Court.

PAOLO V. QUETULIO
Senior State Solicitor
April 19, 2023

SUBSCRIBED AND SWORN TO before me on this 19th day of April 2023, affiant known to me and likewise exhibiting his competent evidence of identity, to wit: IBP ID No. 05658.

JILLIAN MARIE B. CO
State Solicitor

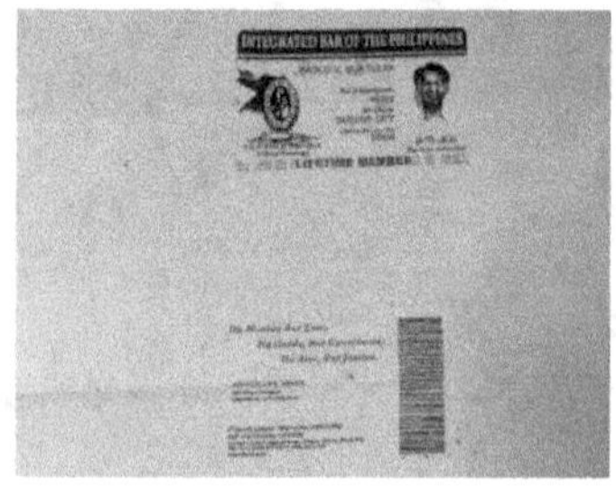

REPUBLIC OF THE PHILIPPINES

AFFIDAVIT OF SERVICE

(Revised as of April 1992)

I, _______________________________ OFFICE OF THE SOLICITOR GENERAL,
with Office address at 134 Amorsolo St., Legaspi Village Makati City, after being sworn to depose and say:

That on ___04/19/2023___, I caused to be served a copy of the following pleading/paper:

NATURE OF THE PLEADING

Manifestation

In case No. _G.R. NO. 263835_, entitled _ELISEO MIJARES RIO, JR., AUGUSTO CASELINA_
VS. COMMISSION ON ELECTIONS, SMARTMATIC TOTAL INFORMATION MANAGEMENT, DITO

pursuant to Section 3,4,5 and 10, Rule 13 of the Rules of Court.

By Personal Service To:

( ) By personally serving to the party or his/her attorney on ___ as shown on p ___
( ) By leaving a copy in his/her clerk or with a person having charge thereof on ___ as shown on p ___

( ) By delivering a copy to the Court/Tribunal Office on ___ as shown on p ___

( ) By depositing copy on ___ in the Post Office at ___ as evidenced by Registry Receipt(s) No.(s) ___ hereto attached and indicated after the name (s) of the addressee(s), and with instruction to the postmaster to return the mail to the sender after (10) days if undelivered.

By Registered Mail To:

Atty. Kalec Justin E. Aguilar
c/o Eliseo Rio, Jr.
Lot 7, Block 11 Soldiers Hill
Barangay Putatan
1722 Muntinlupa City, Philippines

Makati, Metro Manila, Philippines

JOCAS M. NAIDAS, AO 1
GSIS UMID #011-1049-0T35-4

APR 19 2023   (Affiant)

SUBSCRIBED AND SWORN to before me this ___ of ___ at Makati City, Philippines. Affiant exhibiting to me his ___

CATHERINE JOY L. MARCHE-ROMAQUIN
SENIOR STATE SOLICITOR
Solicitor, Officer Administering the Oath
Office of the Solicitor General

23-004756-0019

....

10
JUSTICE IS BOTH THE AIM AND THE YARDSTICK WITH WHICH TO RESOLVE THE CONFLICT. – Da Celestine – May 6, 2023

In this way justice enters into the terrain of contestations about truth. Commitment to truth, at the same time, a demand for justice. As a Patriot, be one to fight for it.
Pls share po XXXinyo. Thanks po.

....

11
Bogus President – Don Azarias
– May 6, 2023

Don Azarias
THE LYING AND TAX-EVADING BOGUS PRESIDENT SO SHAMELESS AND IRREFORMABLE FOR USURPING THE PRESIDENTIAL POWERS AND AUTHORITY THAT HE HAS NO RIGHT TO CARRY OUT.

HEY BBM, HAVE YOU NO SHAME AT ALL? YOU ARE NOT THE DULY-ELECTED PRESIDENT OF THE PHILIPPINES. YOU HAVE NO RIGHT AND AUTHORITY TO REPRESENT THE FILIPINO PEOPLE.

YOU ARE A BOGUS PRESIDENT AND THE WHOLE WORLD KNOWS THAT YOU STOLE THE

ELECTION – THROUGH MACHINATED VCMS AND SD CARDS – FROM LENI ROBREDO WITH THE HELP OF DUTERTE, THE COMELEC AND YOUR POWERFUL ALLIES USING PUBLIC FUNDS TO ATTAIN YOUR SELFISH ENDS.

IN FACT, YOU SHOULD HAVE BEEN PERPETUALLY DISQUALIFIIED FROM RUNNING FOR PUBLIC OFFICE FOR TAX EVASION. AND YOU EVEN HAVE THE NERVES TO TELL THE OVERBURDENED FILIPINO TAXPAYERS TO PAY THEIR TAXES WHEN YOU, YOURSELF, OWE THE BIR P203 BILLION IN UNPAID TAXES.

Maybe we should not wonder anymore about the brazenness of this scumbag. It runs in the family composed of shameless thieves and power-hungry political hacks.

They are true to the end – incorrigible and insatiable gluttons feasting on taxpayers money, public funds and assets.

Don Azarias

Moves to check Beijing's aggressive expansion into the trade routes and strategic islands of the South China Sea will headline talks Monday between President Joe Biden and his Philippines counterpart Ferdinand Marcos at the White House.

....

12
Simple Logic to Understand Rigging of Elections – Eliseo Rio Jr. – May 8, 2023

Here are numerous documents all coming from COMELEC, any one of which can prove that the 2022 Election was RIGGED. One need not be an IT expert to understand this. It only needs SIMPLE LOGIC AND COMMON SENSE.

I for one will not TOLERATE this. Let me put that on record. But if we as a people tolerate this blatant violation of our basic right of suffrage, then we deserve the government we get NOW AND IN THE FUTURE. We deserve the reputation that the world has given us.

We have to stop tolerating this! What we are ACTUALLY DOING is that because we lack the courage or concern to fight against these wrongdoings, we are simply passing the shame to the next generations for them to fix these themselves. And when they do, and surely they would, we will be remembered in history as the generation that tolerated injustice because we just thought of our personal interests and not of the National Interests.

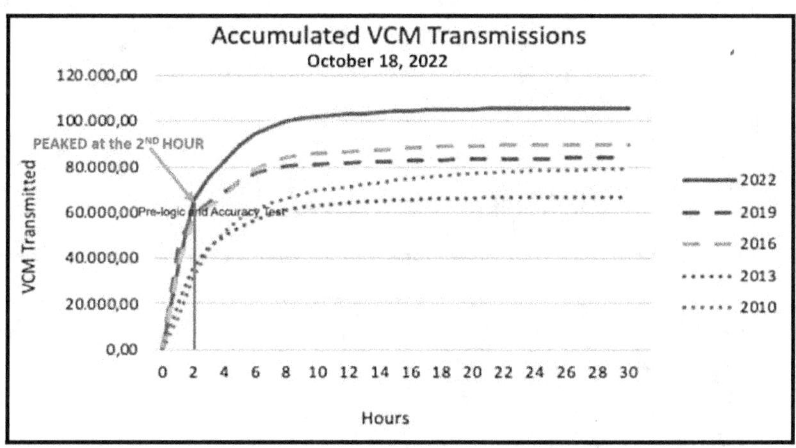

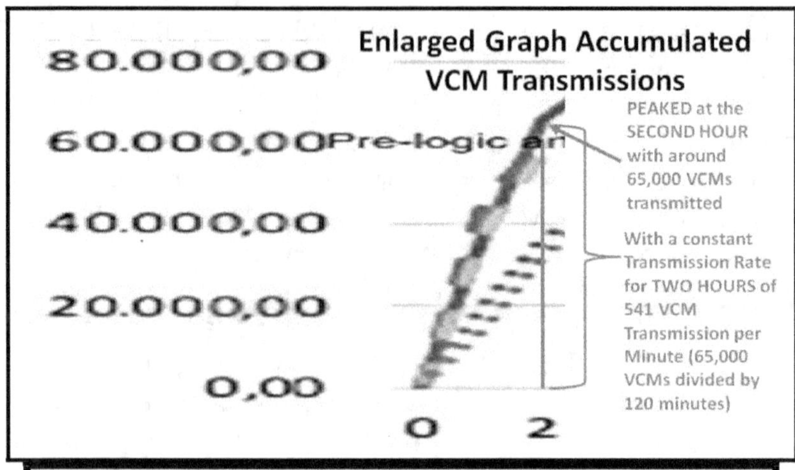

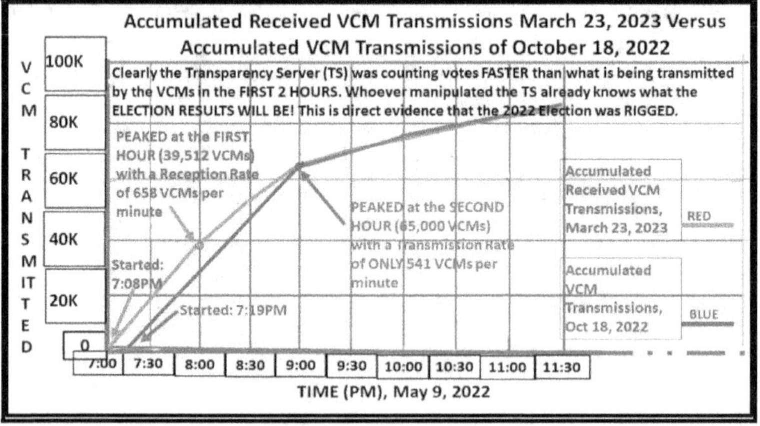

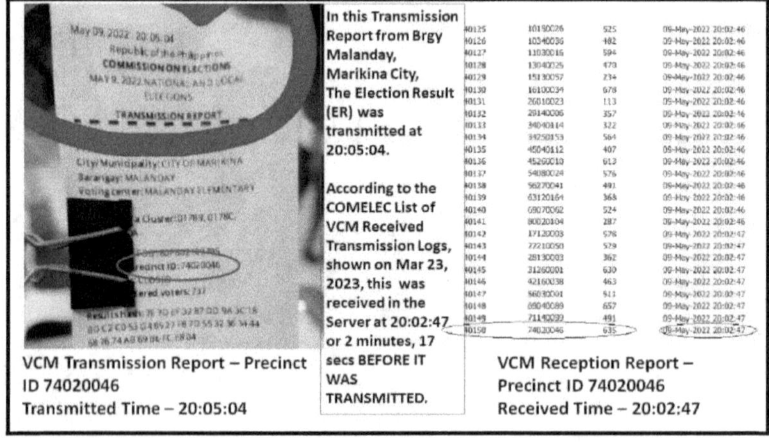

40125	10190026	525	09-May-2022 20:02:46
40126	10340036	482	09-May-2022 20:02:46
40127	11030016	594	09-May-2022 20:02:46
40128	13040025	470	09-May-2022 20:02:46
40129	15130057	234	09-May-2022 20:02:46
40130	16100034	678	09-May-2022 20:02:46
40131	26010023	113	09-May-2022 20:02:46
40132	28140006	357	09-May-2022 20:02:16
40133	34040144	322	09-May-2022 20:02:46
40134	34250153	564	09-May-2022 20:02:46
40135	45040112	407	09-May-2022 20:02:46
40136	45260010	613	09-May-2022 20:02:46
40137	54080024	576	09-May-2022 20:02:46
40138	56270041	491	09-May-2022 20:02:46
40139	63120164	368	09-May-2022 20:02:46
40140	69070062	524	09-May-2022 20:02:46
40141	80020104	287	09-May-2022 20:02:46
40142	17120003	576	09-May-2022 20:02:47
40143	72210050	579	09-May-2022 20:02:47
40144	28130003	362	09-May-2022 20:02:47
40145	31260001	630	09-May-2022 20:02:47
40146	42160038	463	09-May-2022 20:02:47
40147	56080001	511	09-May-2022 20:02:47
40148	69040089	657	09-May-2022 20:02:47
40149	71140000	491	09-May-2022 20:02:47
40150	74020046	635	09-May-2022 20:02:47

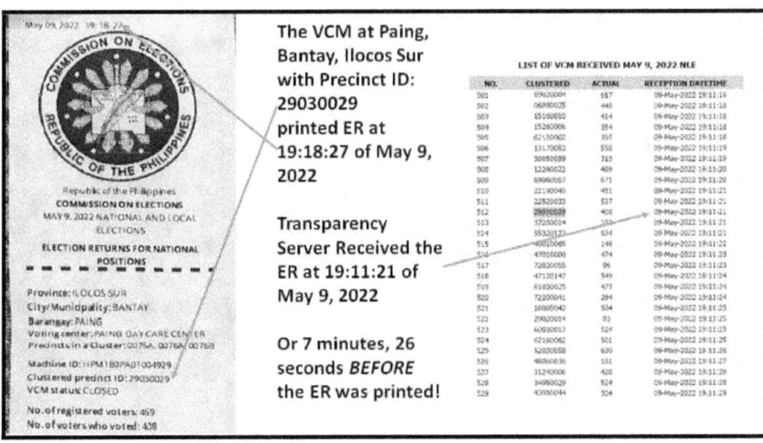

The VCM at Paing, Bantay, Ilocos Sur with Precinct ID: 29030029 printed ER at 19:18:27 of May 9, 2022

Transparency Server Received the ER at 19:11:21 of May 9, 2022

Or 7 minutes, 26 seconds *BEFORE* the ER was printed!

LIST OF VCM RECEIVED MAY 9, 2022 NLE

NO.	CLUSTERED	ACTUAL	RECEPTION DATETIME
501	69020004	617	09-May-2022 19:11:18
502	06090025	448	09-May-2022 19:11:18
503	15160010	414	09-May-2022 19:11:18
504	15260006	384	09-May-2022 19:11:18
505	62150002	365	09-May-2022 19:11:18
506	13170063	558	09-May-2022 19:11:19
507	38050039	313	09-May-2022 19:11:19
508	12290022	409	09-May-2022 19:11:20
509	89060057	671	09-May-2022 19:11:20
510	22190040	451	09-May-2022 19:11:21
511	22520033	527	09-May-2022 19:11:21
512	29030029	408	09-May-2022 19:11:21
513	57250014	103	09-May-2022 19:11:21
514	55320123	534	09-May-2022 19:11:21
515	48010065	146	09-May-2022 19:11:22
516	47010000	474	09-May-2022 19:11:23
517	72020055	96	09-May-2022 19:11:23
518	47120147	549	09-May-2022 19:11:24
519	61030025	471	09-May-2022 19:11:24
520	72200041	264	09-May-2022 19:11:25
521	16060042	504	09-May-2022 19:11:25
522	29020014	81	09-May-2022 19:11:25
523	60930013	524	09-May-2022 19:11:25
524	62160062	501	09-May-2022 19:11:25
525	52020058	636	09-May-2022 19:11:26
526	48060036	181	09-May-2022 19:11:27
527	31240006	428	09-May-2022 19:11:28
528	34980029	524	09-May-2022 19:11:28
529	43060044	324	09-May-2022 19:11:29

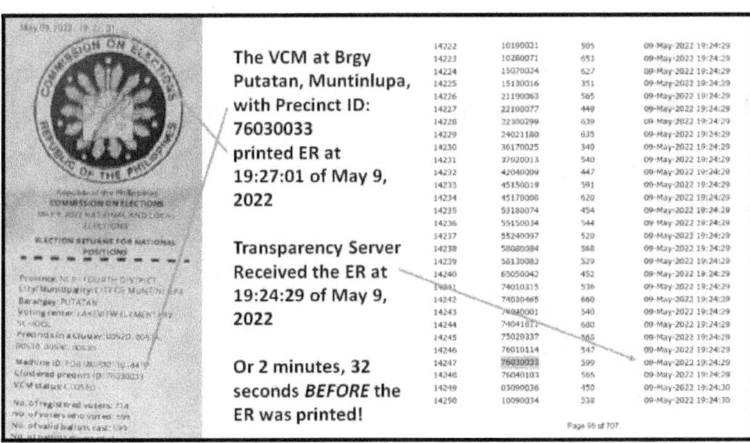

The VCM at Brgy Putatan, Muntinlupa, with Precinct ID: 76030033 printed ER at 19:27:01 of May 9, 2022

Transparency Server Received the ER at 19:24:29 of May 9, 2022

Or 2 minutes, 32 seconds *BEFORE* the ER was printed!

14222	10190021	505	09-May-2022 19:24:29
14223	10280071	653	09-May-2022 19:24:29
14224	15070024	627	09-May-2022 19:24:29
14225	15130016	351	09-May-2022 19:24:29
14226	21190063	565	09-May-2022 19:24:29
14227	22100077	449	09-May-2022 19:24:29
14228	22300299	639	09-May-2022 19:24:29
14229	24021180	635	09-May-2022 19:24:29
14230	36170025	340	09-May-2022 19:24:29
14231	37020013	540	09-May-2022 19:24:29
14232	42040009	447	09-May-2022 19:24:29
14233	45150019	591	09-May-2022 19:24:29
14234	45170008	620	09-May-2022 19:24:29
14235	53180074	454	09-May-2022 19:24:29
14236	55150034	544	09-May-2022 19:24:29
14237	55240097	520	09-May-2023 19:24:29
14238	58080084	568	09-May-2022 19:24:29
14239	58130083	329	09-May-2022 19:24:29
14240	65050042	452	09-May-2022 19:24:29
14241	74010315	536	09-May-2022 19:24:29
14242	74030465	660	09-May-2022 19:24:29
14243	74040001	540	09-May-2022 19:24:29
14244	74041612	680	09-May-2022 19:24:29
14245	75020337	568	09-May-2022 19:24:29
14246	76010114	547	09-May-2022 19:24:29
14247	76030033	599	09-May-2022 19:24:29
14248	76040103	565	09-May-2022 19:24:29
14249	03090036	450	09-May-2022 19:24:30
14250	10090034	538	09-May-2022 19:24:30

Page 95 of 707

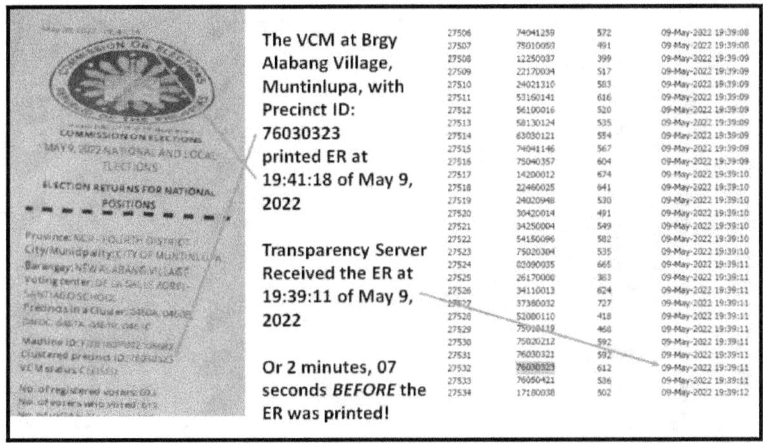

The VCM at Brgy Alabang Village, Muntinlupa, with Precinct ID: 76030323 printed ER at 19:41:18 of May 9, 2022

Transparency Server Received the ER at 19:39:11 of May 9, 2022

Or 2 minutes, 07 seconds *BEFORE* the ER was printed!

27506	74041259	572	09-May-2022 19:39:08
27507	75010050	491	09-May-2022 19:39:08
27508	12250037	399	09-May-2022 19:39:09
27509	22170004	517	09-May-2022 19:39:09
27510	24021310	583	09-May-2022 19:39:09
27511	53160141	616	09-May-2022 19:39:09
27512	56100016	520	09-May-2022 19:39:09
27513	58130124	535	09-May-2022 19:39:09
27514	63030121	554	09-May-2022 19:39:09
27515	74041146	567	09-May-2022 19:39:09
27516	75040357	604	09-May-2022 19:39:09
27517	14200012	674	09-May-2022 19:39:10
27518	22460025	641	09-May-2022 19:39:10
27519	24020948	530	09-May-2022 19:39:10
27520	30420014	491	09-May-2022 19:39:10
27521	34250004	549	09-May-2022 19:39:10
27522	54150096	582	09-May-2022 19:39:10
27523	75020304	535	09-May-2022 19:39:10
27524	02090035	665	09-May-2022 19:39:11
27525	26170000	383	09-May-2022 19:39:11
27526	34110013	624	09-May-2022 19:39:11
27527	37380032	727	09-May-2022 19:39:11
27528	52080110	418	09-May-2022 19:39:11
27529	75010419	468	09-May-2022 19:39:11
27530	75020212	592	09-May-2022 19:39:11
27531	76030321	592	09-May-2022 19:39:11
27532	76030323	612	09-May-2022 19:39:11
27533	76050421	536	09-May-2022 19:39:11
27534	17180038	502	09-May-2022 19:39:12

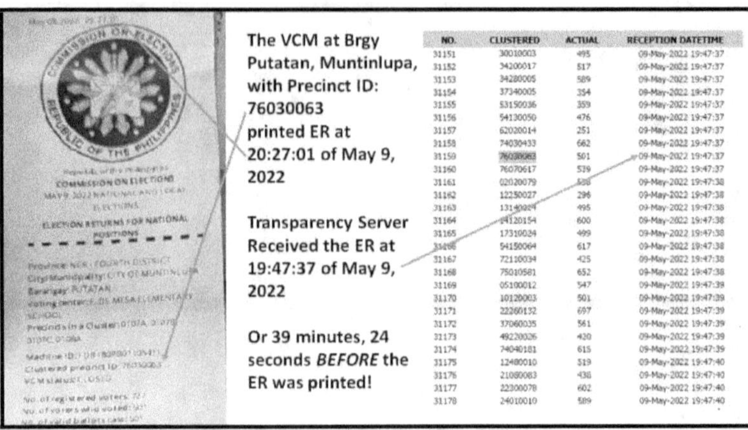

The VCM at Brgy Putatan, Muntinlupa, with Precinct ID: 76030063 printed ER at 20:27:01 of May 9, 2022

Transparency Server Received the ER at 19:47:37 of May 9, 2022

Or 39 minutes, 24 seconds *BEFORE* the ER was printed!

NO.	CLUSTERED	ACTUAL	RECEPTION DATETIME
31151	30010003	495	09-May-2022 19:47:37
31152	34200017	517	09-May-2022 19:47:37
31153	34280005	589	09-May-2022 19:47:37
31154	37340005	354	09-May-2022 19:47:37
31155	53150036	359	09-May-2022 19:47:37
31156	54130050	476	09-May-2022 19:47:37
31157	62020014	251	09-May-2022 19:47:37
31158	74030433	662	09-May-2022 19:47:37
31159	76030063	501	09-May-2022 19:47:37
31160	76070617	539	09-May-2022 19:47:37
31161	02020079	538	09-May-2022 19:47:38
31162	12250027	296	09-May-2022 19:47:38
31163	13140024	495	09-May-2022 19:47:38
31164	14120154	600	09-May-2022 19:47:38
31165	17310024	499	09-May-2022 19:47:38
31166	54150064	617	09-May-2022 19:47:38
31167	72110034	425	09-May-2022 19:47:38
31168	75010581	652	09-May-2022 19:47:38
31169	05100012	547	09-May-2022 19:47:39
31170	10120003	501	09-May-2022 19:47:39
31171	22260132	697	09-May-2022 19:47:39
31172	37060035	561	09-May-2022 19:47:39
31173	49220026	420	09-May-2022 19:47:39
31174	74040181	615	09-May-2022 19:47:39
31175	12480010	519	09-May-2022 19:47:40
31176	21080083	438	09-May-2022 19:47:40
31177	22300078	602	09-May-2022 19:47:40
31178	24010010	589	09-May-2022 19:47:40

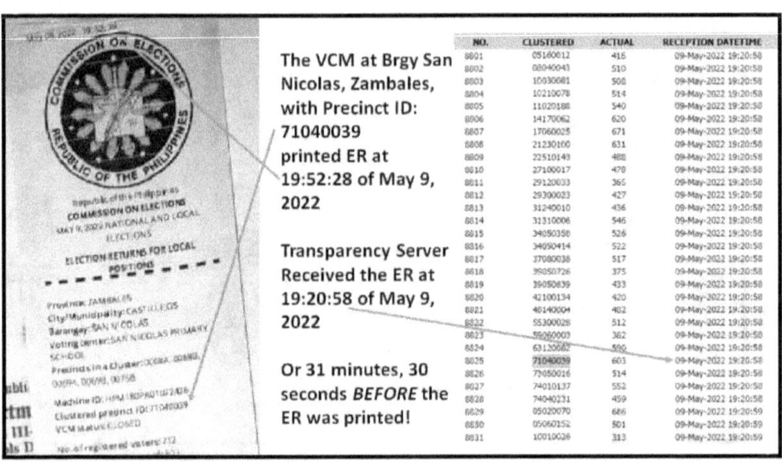

The VCM at Brgy San Nicolas, Zambales, with Precinct ID: 71040039 printed ER at 19:52:28 of May 9, 2022

Transparency Server Received the ER at 19:20:58 of May 9, 2022

Or 31 minutes, 30 seconds *BEFORE* the ER was printed!

NO.	CLUSTERED	ACTUAL	RECEPTION DATETIME
8801	05160012	418	09-May-2022 19:20:58
8802	08040043	510	09-May-2022 19:20:58
8803	10030081	500	09-May-2022 19:20:58
8804	10210078	514	09-May-2022 19:20:58
8805	11020188	540	09-May-2022 19:20:58
8806	14170062	620	09-May-2022 19:20:58
8807	17060025	671	09-May-2022 19:20:58
8808	21230100	631	09-May-2022 19:20:58
8809	22510143	488	09-May-2022 19:20:58
8810	27100017	478	09-May-2022 19:20:58
8811	29120033	365	09-May-2022 19:20:58
8812	29300023	427	09-May-2022 19:20:58
8813	31240010	436	09-May-2022 19:20:58
8814	31310006	546	09-May-2022 19:20:58
8815	34050358	526	09-May-2022 19:20:58
8816	34090414	522	09-May-2022 19:20:58
8817	37080038	517	09-May-2022 19:20:58
8818	39050726	375	09-May-2022 19:20:58
8819	39050839	433	09-May-2022 19:20:58
8820	42100134	420	09-May-2022 19:20:58
8821	48140004	482	09-May-2022 19:20:58
8822	55300028	512	09-May-2022 19:20:58
8823	59060003	362	09-May-2022 19:20:58
8824	63120062	590	09-May-2022 19:20:58
8825	71040039	603	09-May-2022 19:20:58
8826	73050016	514	09-May-2022 19:20:58
8827	74010137	552	09-May-2022 19:20:58
8828	74040231	459	09-May-2022 19:20:58
8829	05020070	686	09-May-2022 19:20:59
8830	05060152	501	09-May-2022 19:20:59
8831	10010026	313	09-May-2022 19:20:59

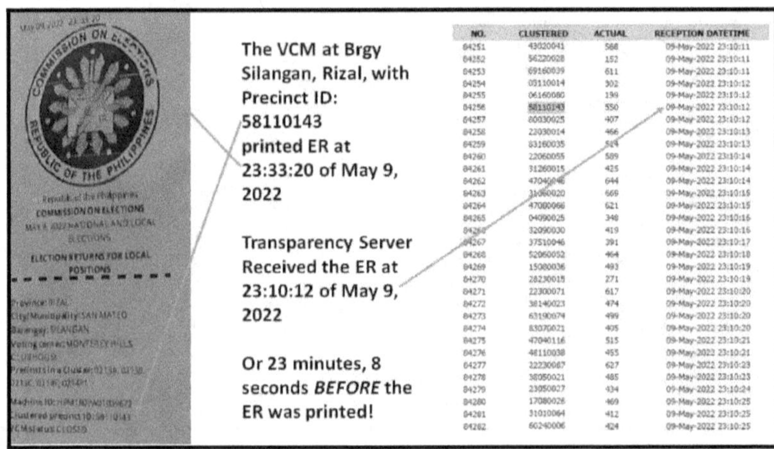

The VCM at Brgy Silangan, Rizal, with Precinct ID: 58110143 printed ER at 23:33:20 of May 9, 2022

Transparency Server Received the ER at 23:10:12 of May 9, 2022

Or 23 minutes, 8 seconds *BEFORE* the ER was printed!

NO.	CLUSTERED	ACTUAL	RECEPTION DATETIME
04251	43020041	588	09-May-2022 23:10:11
04252	56220028	152	09-May-2022 23:10:11
04253	69160039	611	09-May-2022 23:10:11
04254	03110014	302	09-May-2022 23:10:12
04255	06160080	199	09-May-2022 23:10:12
04256	58110143	550	09-May-2022 23:10:12
04257	80030025	407	09-May-2022 23:10:12
04258	22030014	466	09-May-2022 23:10:13
04259	83160035	549	09-May-2022 23:10:13
04260	22060055	589	09-May-2022 23:10:14
04261	31260015	425	09-May-2022 23:10:14
04262	47040046	644	09-May-2022 23:10:14
04263	31060020	669	09-May-2022 23:10:15
04264	47000066	621	09-May-2022 23:10:15
04265	04090025	348	09-May-2022 23:10:16
04266	32090030	419	09-May-2022 23:10:16
04267	37510046	391	09-May-2022 23:10:17
04268	52060052	464	09-May-2022 23:10:18
04269	15080036	493	09-May-2022 23:10:19
04270	28230015	271	09-May-2022 23:10:19
04271	22300071	617	09-May-2022 23:10:20
04272	38140023	474	09-May-2022 23:10:20
04273	63190074	499	09-May-2022 23:10:20
04274	83070021	405	09-May-2022 23:10:20
04275	47040116	515	09-May-2022 23:10:21
04276	48110038	455	09-May-2022 23:10:21
04277	22230067	627	09-May-2022 23:10:23
04278	38050021	485	09-May-2022 23:10:23
04279	23050027	434	09-May-2022 23:10:24
04280	17080026	469	09-May-2022 23:10:25
04281	31010064	412	09-May-2022 23:10:25
04282	60240006	424	09-May-2022 23:10:25

The VCM at Brgy San Andres, Tarlac, with Precinct ID: 69170045 printed ER at 22:03:39 of May 9, 2022

Transparency Server Received the ER at 20:04:20 of May 9, 2022

Or 1 hour, 59 minutes, 19 seconds *BEFORE* the ER was printed!

41377	37020014	424	09-May-2022 20:04:19
41378	37030043	692	09-May-2022 20:04:19
41379	65110001	480	09-May-2022 20:04:19
41380	69080023	301	09-May-2022 20:04:19
41381	73320067	567	09-May-2022 20:04:19
41382	76020197	552	09-May-2022 20:04:19
41383	76020480	523	09-May-2022 20:04:19
41384	10140054	527	09-May-2022 20:04:20
41385	22050032	499	09-May-2022 20:04:20
41386	22320060	593	09-May-2022 20:04:20
41387	34060024	497	09-May-2022 20:04:20
41388	43050164	673	09-May-2022 20:04:20
41389	49080056	467	09-May-2022 20:04:20
41390	49300009	434	09-May-2022 20:04:20
41391	53180061	342	09-May-2022 20:04:20
41392	55110073	378	09-May-2022 20:04:20
41393	55460142	475	09-May-2022 20:04:20
41394	58030006	560	09-May-2022 20:04:20
41395	60070045	108	09-May-2022 20:04:20
41396	64060027	572	09-May-2022 20:04:20
41397	69070051	533	09-May-2022 20:04:20
41398	69170045	601	09-May-2022 20:04:20
41399	70020032	658	09-May-2022 20:04:20
41400	80070108	311	09-May-2022 20:04:20

Page 276 of 707

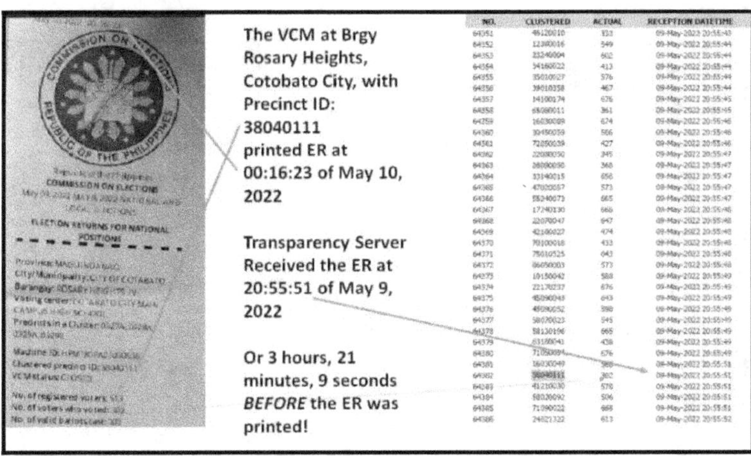

The VCM at Brgy Rosary Heights, Cotobato City, with Precinct ID: 38040111 printed ER at 00:16:23 of May 10, 2022

Transparency Server Received the ER at 20:55:51 of May 9, 2022

Or 3 hours, 21 minutes, 9 seconds *BEFORE* the ER was printed!

NO.	CLUSTERED	ACTUAL	RECEPTION DATETIME
64351	46120010	133	09-May-2022 20:55:43
64352	12380016	549	09-May-2022 20:55:44
64353	23240004	602	09-May-2022 20:55:44
64354	34160022	413	09-May-2022 20:55:44
64355	35010027	576	09-May-2022 20:55:44
64356	39010358	467	09-May-2022 20:55:44
64357	14100174	676	09-May-2022 20:55:45
64358	68080011	361	09-May-2022 20:55:45
64359	16030008	624	09-May-2022 20:55:46
64360	30450059	566	09-May-2022 20:55:46
64361	72050039	427	09-May-2022 20:55:46
64362	22080050	345	09-May-2022 20:55:47
64363	28090090	368	09-May-2022 20:55:47
64364	33140015	656	09-May-2022 20:55:47
64365	47020057	573	09-May-2022 20:55:47
64366	55240073	665	09-May-2022 20:55:47
64367	17240130	666	09-May-2022 20:55:48
64368	22070047	647	09-May-2022 20:55:48
64369	42100027	474	09-May-2022 20:55:48
64370	70100018	433	09-May-2022 20:55:48
64371	75010525	043	09-May-2022 20:55:48
64372	06050003	573	09-May-2022 20:55:48
64373	19150042	588	09-May-2022 20:55:49
64374	22170237	676	09-May-2022 20:55:49
64375	45090048	643	09-May-2022 20:55:49
64376	48090052	398	09-May-2022 20:55:49
64377	58020023	545	09-May-2022 20:55:49
64378	58130196	665	09-May-2022 20:55:49
64379	63180041	438	09-May-2022 20:55:49
64380	71050004	576	09-May-2022 20:55:49
64381	16030049	985	09-May-2022 20:55:51
64382	38040111	302	09-May-2022 20:55:51
64383	41210030	578	09-May-2022 20:55:51
64384	58020092	506	09-May-2022 20:55:51
64385	71090022	665	09-May-2022 20:55:51
64386	24021322	613	09-May-2022 20:55:52

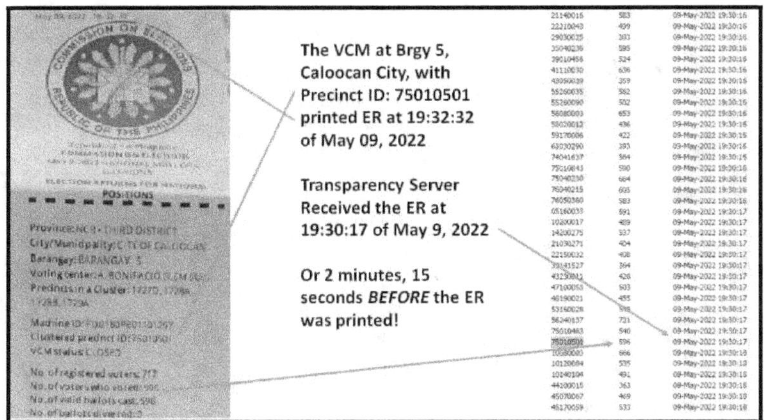

The VCM at Brgy 5, Caloocan City, with Precinct ID: 75010501 printed ER at 19:32:32 of May 09, 2022

Transparency Server Received the ER at 19:30:17 of May 9, 2022

Or 2 minutes, 15 seconds *BEFORE* the ER was printed!

CLUSTERED	ACTUAL	RECEPTION DATETIME
21140016	583	09-May-2022 19:30:16
22210043	499	09-May-2022 19:30:16
29030025	303	09-May-2022 19:30:16
35040236	595	09-May-2022 19:30:16
29010456	324	09-May-2022 19:30:16
41110030	636	09-May-2022 19:30:16
43050019	259	09-May-2022 19:30:16
55260035	582	09-May-2022 19:30:16
55260090	502	09-May-2022 19:30:16
58080003	653	09-May-2022 19:30:16
58020012	436	09-May-2022 19:30:16
59170006	422	09-May-2022 19:30:15
63030290	393	09-May-2022 19:30:15
74041637	564	09-May-2022 19:30:15
75010843	590	09-May-2022 19:30:16
75040230	664	09-May-2022 19:30:16
75040215	605	09-May-2022 19:30:16
76050340	583	09-May-2022 19:30:16
05180033	591	09-May-2022 19:30:17
10200017	489	09-May-2022 19:30:17
14200275	537	09-May-2022 19:30:17
21090271	404	09-May-2022 19:30:17
22150032	408	09-May-2022 19:30:17
39141527	364	09-May-2022 19:30:17
43230012	428	09-May-2022 19:30:17
47100053	603	09-May-2022 19:30:17
46190021	455	09-May-2022 19:30:17
53160028	598	09-May-2022 19:30:17
56240137	721	09-May-2022 19:30:17
75010443	540	09-May-2022 19:30:17
75010501	596	09-May-2022 19:30:17
10200005	666	09-May-2022 19:30:18
10120004	535	09-May-2022 19:30:18
10140104	491	09-May-2022 19:30:18
44200015	363	09-May-2022 19:30:18
45070067	469	09-May-2022 19:30:18
46170059	533	09-May-2022 19:30:18

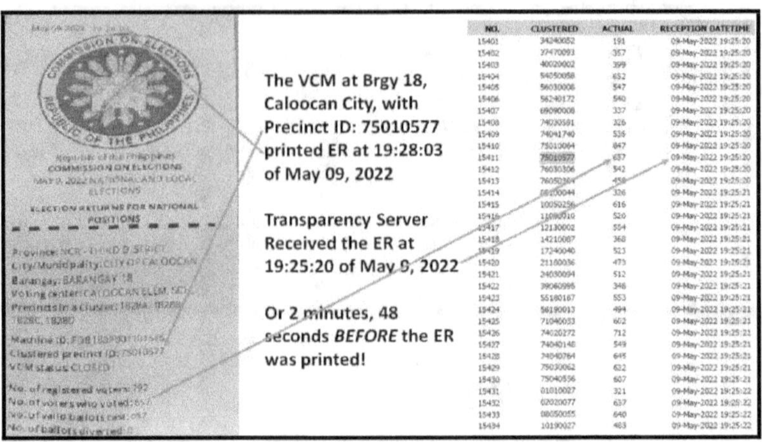

NO.	CLUSTERED	ACTUAL	RECEPTION DATETIME
15401	34240052	191	09-May-2022 19:25:20
15402	37470093	357	09-May-2022 19:25:20
15403	40020002	399	09-May-2022 19:25:20
15404	54050058	652	09-May-2022 19:25:20
15405	56030006	547	09-May-2022 19:25:20
15406	56240172	540	09-May-2022 19:25:20
15407	69090008	337	09-May-2022 19:25:20
15408	74020581	326	09-May-2022 19:25:20
15409	74041740	536	09-May-2022 19:25:20
15410	75010064	847	09-May-2022 19:25:20
15411	75010577	637	09-May-2022 19:25:20
15412	76030306	542	09-May-2022 19:25:20
15413	76050364	458	09-May-2022 19:25:20
15414	88200044	326	09-May-2022 19:25:21
15415	10050256	616	09-May-2022 19:25:21
15416	11090010	520	09-May-2022 19:25:21
15417	12130002	554	09-May-2022 19:25:21
15418	14210087	368	09-May-2022 19:25:21
15419	17240040	523	09-May-2022 19:25:21
15420	21100036	473	09-May-2022 19:25:21
15421	24030094	512	09-May-2022 19:25:21
15422	39060996	348	09-May-2022 19:25:21
15423	55180167	553	09-May-2022 19:25:21
15424	56190013	494	09-May-2022 19:25:21
15425	71040053	602	09-May-2022 19:25:21
15426	74020272	712	09-May-2022 19:25:21
15427	74040148	549	09-May-2022 19:25:21
15428	74040764	645	09-May-2022 19:25:21
15429	75030062	632	09-May-2022 19:25:21
15430	75040556	607	09-May-2022 19:25:21
15431	01010027	321	09-May-2022 19:25:22
15432	02020077	637	09-May-2022 19:25:22
15433	08050055	640	09-May-2022 19:25:22
15434	10190027	483	09-May-2022 19:25:22

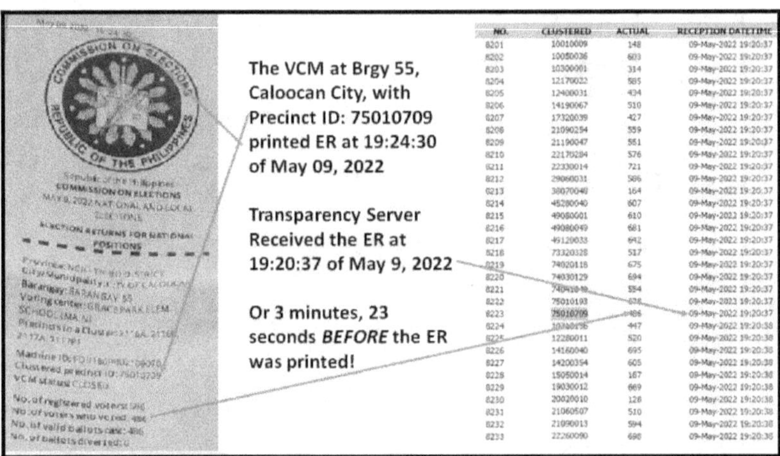

NO.	CLUSTERED	ACTUAL	RECEPTION DATETIME
8201	10010009	148	09-May-2022 19:20:37
8202	10050036	603	09-May-2022 19:20:37
8203	10300001	314	09-May-2022 19:20:37
8204	12170022	585	09-May-2022 19:20:37
8205	12400031	434	09-May-2022 19:20:37
8206	14190067	510	09-May-2022 19:20:37
8207	17320039	427	09-May-2022 19:20:37
8208	21090254	559	09-May-2022 19:20:37
8209	21190047	551	09-May-2022 19:20:37
8210	22170284	576	09-May-2022 19:20:37
8211	22330014	721	09-May-2022 19:20:37
8212	29060031	586	09-May-2022 19:20:37
8213	38070049	164	09-May-2022 19:20:37
8214	45280040	607	09-May-2022 19:20:37
8215	49080001	610	09-May-2022 19:20:37
8216	49080049	681	09-May-2022 19:20:37
8217	49120033	642	09-May-2022 19:20:37
8218	73320328	517	09-May-2022 19:20:37
8219	74020118	675	09-May-2022 19:20:37
8220	74030129	694	09-May-2022 19:20:37
8221	74041040	554	09-May-2022 19:20:37
8222	75010193	638	09-May-2022 19:20:37
8223	75010709	486	09-May-2022 19:20:37
8224	10340196	447	09-May-2022 19:20:38
8225	12280011	520	09-May-2022 19:20:38
8226	14160040	695	09-May-2022 19:20:38
8227	14200394	605	09-May-2022 19:20:38
8228	15050014	167	09-May-2022 19:20:38
8229	19030012	669	09-May-2022 19:20:38
8230	20020010	128	09-May-2022 19:20:38
8231	21060507	510	09-May-2022 19:20:38
8232	21090013	594	09-May-2022 19:20:38
8233	22260090	698	09-May-2022 19:20:38

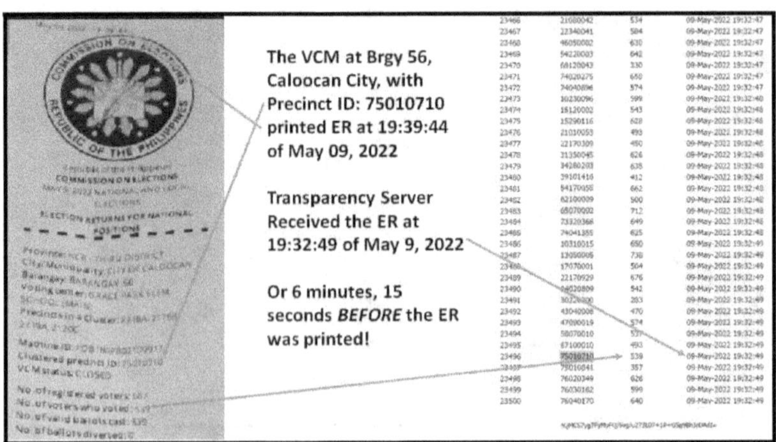

NO.	CLUSTERED	ACTUAL	RECEPTION DATETIME
23466	21080042	534	09-May-2022 19:32:47
23467	22340041	584	09-May-2022 19:32:47
23468	46050002	630	09-May-2022 19:32:47
23469	54220003	642	09-May-2022 19:32:47
23470	68120043	330	09-May-2022 19:32:47
23471	74020275	650	09-May-2022 19:32:47
23472	74040896	574	09-May-2022 19:32:47
23473	16230096	599	09-May-2022 19:32:48
23474	18120002	543	09-May-2022 19:32:48
23475	15290116	628	09-May-2022 19:32:48
23476	21010053	493	09-May-2022 19:32:48
23477	22170309	450	09-May-2022 19:32:48
23478	31350045	626	09-May-2022 19:32:48
23479	34280203	635	09-May-2022 19:32:48
23480	39101416	412	09-May-2022 19:32:48
23481	54170058	662	09-May-2022 19:32:48
23482	62100009	500	09-May-2022 19:32:48
23483	68070002	712	09-May-2022 19:32:48
23484	73320368	649	09-May-2022 19:32:48
23485	74041355	625	09-May-2022 19:32:48
23486	10310015	650	09-May-2022 19:32:49
23487	13090006	738	09-May-2022 19:32:49
23488	17070001	504	09-May-2022 19:32:49
23489	22170929	676	09-May-2022 19:32:49
23490	04020809	542	09-May-2022 19:32:49
23491	30220900	283	09-May-2022 19:32:49
23492	43040008	470	09-May-2022 19:32:49
23493	47090019	574	09-May-2022 19:32:49
23494	58070010	527	09-May-2022 19:32:49
23495	67100010	493	09-May-2022 19:32:49
23496	75010710	539	09-May-2022 19:32:49
23497	75010641	357	09-May-2022 19:32:49
23498	76020349	626	09-May-2022 19:32:49
23499	76030162	599	09-May-2022 19:32:49
23500	76040170	640	09-May-2022 19:32:49

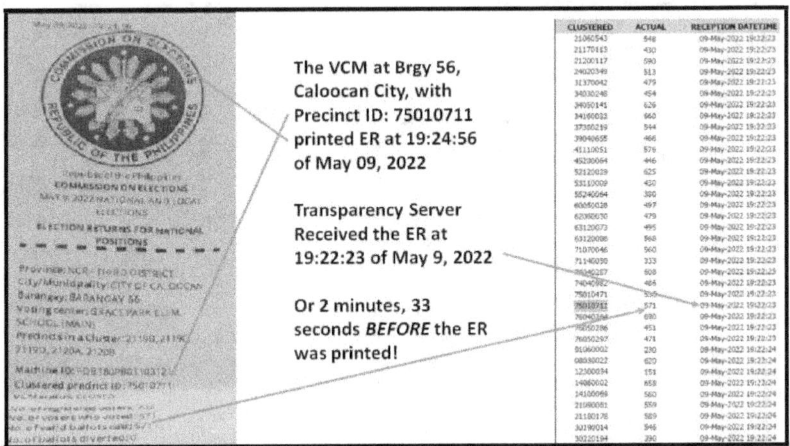

The VCM at Brgy 56, Caloocan City, with Precinct ID: 75010711 printed ER at 19:24:56 of May 09, 2022

Transparency Server Received the ER at 19:22:23 of May 9, 2022

Or 2 minutes, 33 seconds *BEFORE* the ER was printed!

CLUSTERED	ACTUAL	RECEPTION DATETIME
21060543	548	09-May-2022 19:22:23
21170163	430	09-May-2022 19:22:23
21200117	590	09-May-2022 19:22:23
24020349	513	09-May-2022 19:22:23
31370042	479	09-May-2022 19:21:23
34030248	454	09-May-2022 19:22:23
34090141	626	09-May-2022 19:22:23
34160033	960	09-May-2022 19:22:23
37360219	544	09-May-2022 19:22:23
39040655	466	09-May-2022 19:22:23
41110051	576	09-May-2022 19:22:23
45200064	446	09-May-2022 19:22:23
52120039	625	09-May-2022 19:22:23
53110009	430	09-May-2022 19:22:23
55240064	380	09-May-2022 19:22:23
60050028	497	09-May-2022 19:22:23
62060070	479	09-May-2022 19:22:23
63120073	495	09-May-2022 19:22:23
63120086	568	09-May-2022 19:22:23
71070046	560	09-May-2022 19:22:23
71140090	353	09-May-2022 19:22:23
74040267	608	09-May-2022 19:22:23
74040982	486	09-May-2022 19:22:23
75010471	539	09-May-2022 19:22:23
75010711	571	09-May-2022 19:22:23
76040184	690	09-May-2022 19:22:23
76050286	451	09-May-2022 19:22:23
76050297	471	09-May-2022 19:22:23
81060002	230	09-May-2022 19:22:24
08030022	620	09-May-2022 19:23:24
12300034	151	09-May-2022 19:22:24
14060002	658	09-May-2022 19:23:24
14160069	560	09-May-2022 19:22:24
21080081	559	09-May-2022 19:22:24
21180178	589	09-May-2022 19:22:24
30190014	546	09-May-2022 19:22:24
30220194	390	09-May-2022 19:22:24

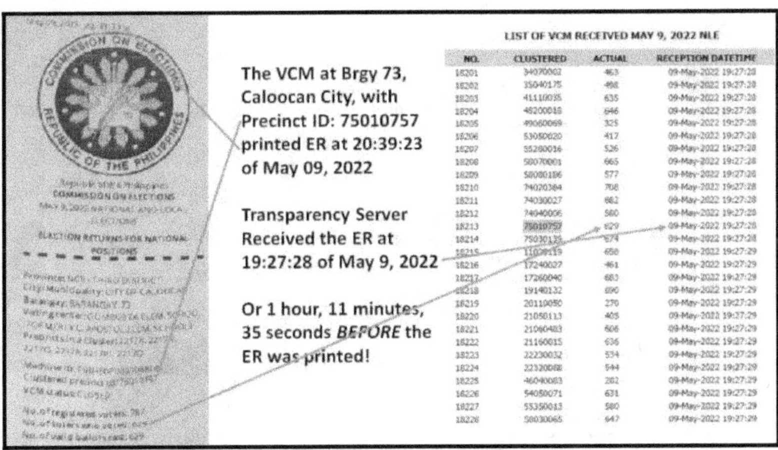

The VCM at Brgy 73, Caloocan City, with Precinct ID: 75010757 printed ER at 20:39:23 of May 09, 2022

Transparency Server Received the ER at 19:27:28 of May 9, 2022

Or 1 hour, 11 minutes, 35 seconds *BEFORE* the ER was printed!

LIST OF VCM RECEIVED MAY 9, 2022 NLE

NO.	CLUSTERED	ACTUAL	RECEPTION DATETIME
18201	34070002	463	09-May-2022 19:27:28
18202	35040175	498	09-May-2022 19:27:28
18203	41110035	635	09-May-2022 19:27:28
18204	48200018	646	09-May-2022 19:27:28
18205	49060069	325	09-May-2022 19:27:28
18206	53050020	417	09-May-2022 19:27:28
18207	55280016	526	09-May-2022 19:27:28
18208	58070001	665	09-May-2022 19:27:28
18209	58080186	577	09-May-2022 19:27:28
18210	74020304	708	09-May-2022 19:27:28
18211	74030027	682	09-May-2022 19:27:28
18212	74040006	580	09-May-2022 19:27:28
18213	75010757	829	09-May-2022 19:27:28
18214	75030125	674	09-May-2022 19:27:28
18215	11030119	658	09-May-2022 19:27:29
18216	17240027	461	09-May-2022 19:27:29
18217	17260040	683	09-May-2022 19:27:29
18218	19140132	690	09-May-2022 19:27:29
18219	20110050	270	09-May-2022 19:27:29
18220	21050113	405	09-May-2022 19:27:29
18221	21060483	606	09-May-2022 19:27:29
18222	21160015	636	09-May-2022 19:27:29
18223	22230032	534	09-May-2022 19:27:29
18224	22320088	544	09-May-2022 19:27:29
18225	46040083	282	09-May-2022 19:27:29
18226	54050071	631	09-May-2022 19:27:29
18227	55350013	580	09-May-2022 19:27:29
18228	58030065	647	09-May-2022 19:27:29

The VCM at Brgy 73, Caloocan City, with Precinct ID: 75010753 printed ER at 19:30:32 of May 09, 2022

Transparency Server Received the ER at 19:26:43 of May 9, 2022

Or 3 minutes, 49 seconds *BEFORE* the ER was printed!

NO.	CLUSTERED	ACTUAL	RECEPTION DATETIME
17254	67060020	602	09-May-2022 19:26:42
17255	69090040	564	09-May-2022 19:26:42
17256	74020098	677	09-May-2022 19:26:42
17257	74030051	660	09-May-2022 19:26:42
17258	75040592	580	09-May-2022 19:26:42
17259	76010318	558	09-May-2022 19:26:42
17260	76030301	592	09-May-2022 19:26:42
17261	77060042	522	09-May-2022 19:26:42
17262	03050089	587	09-May-2022 19:26:42
17263	10050044	651	09-May-2022 19:26:43
17264	14060001	663	09-May-2022 19:26:43
17265	24020410	544	09-May-2022 19:26:43
17266	26040034	491	09-May-2022 19:26:43
17267	30340022	528	09-May-2022 19:26:43
17268	34030185	581	09-May-2022 19:26:43
17269	45100010	514	09-May-2022 19:26:43
17270	45200038	546	09-May-2022 19:26:43
17271	47090088	428	09-May-2022 19:26:43
17272	56270046	621	09-May-2022 19:26:43
17273	58020603	557	09-May-2022 19:26:43
17274	62060037	517	09-May-2022 19:26:43
17275	69040111	693	09-May-2022 19:26:43
17276	69260216	555	09-May-2022 19:26:43
17277	74041007	557	09-May-2022 19:26:43
17278	74041716	489	09-May-2022 19:26:43
17279	75010011	637	09-May-2022 19:26:43
17280	75010753	630	09-May-2022 19:26:43
17281	10090121	650	09-May-2022 19:26:44
17282	10110020	374	09-May-2022 19:26:44
17283	13150060	587	09-May-2022 19:26:44
17284	21030139	471	09-May-2022 19:26:44
17285	21050028	486	09-May-2022 19:26:44
17286	29300012	269	09-May-2022 19:26:44

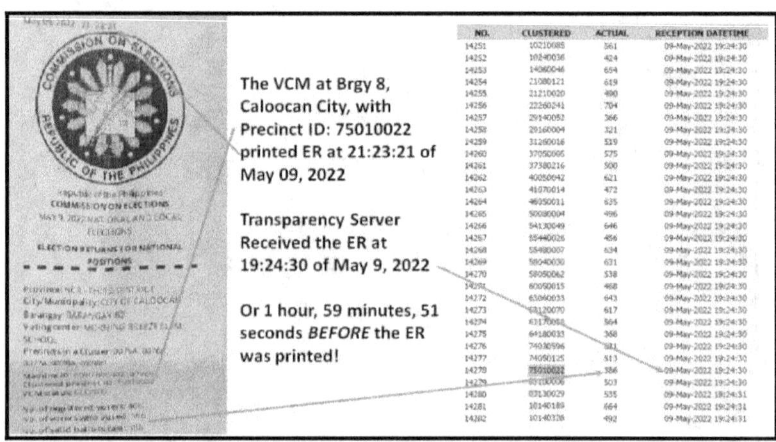

The VCM at Brgy 8, Caloocan City, with Precinct ID: 75010510 printed ER at 20:22:26 of May 09, 2022

Transparency Server Received the ER at 19:22:12 of May 9, 2022

Or 1 hour, 0 minute, 14 seconds *BEFORE* the ER was printed!

NO.	CLUSTERED	ACTUAL	RECEPTION DATETIME
10815	17230075	510	09-May-2022 19:22:12
10816	21140034	384	09-May-2022 19:22:12
10817	21180043	487	09-May-2022 19:22:12
10818	21200126	587	09-May-2022 19:22:12
10819	22170012	520	09-May-2022 19:22:12
10820	24021376	544	09-May-2022 19:22:12
10821	30220046	545	09-May-2022 19:22:12
10822	31150058	413	09-May-2022 19:22:12
10823	31370014	444	09-May-2022 19:22:12
10824	35120001	604	09-May-2022 19:22:12
10825	37480050	363	09-May-2022 19:22:12
10826	45090034	587	09-May-2022 19:22:12
10827	52060050	570	09-May-2022 19:22:12
10828	55180101	537	09-May-2022 19:22:12
10829	55190024	539	09-May-2022 19:22:12
10830	55390025	633	09-May-2022 19:22:12
10831	58100029	606	09-May-2022 19:22:12
10832	60050036	610	09-May-2022 19:22:12
10833	63170045	387	09-May-2022 19:22:12
10834	67240058	623	09-May-2022 19:22:12
10835	68150006	505	09-May-2022 19:22:12
10836	68180007	665	09-May-2022 19:22:12
10837	72020075	450	09-May-2022 19:22:12
10838	72070007	575	09-May-2022 19:22:12
10839	74010149	632	09-May-2022 19:22:12
10840	75010166	633	09-May-2022 19:22:12
10841	75010505	512	09-May-2022 19:22:12
10842	75010510	667	09-May-2022 19:22:12
10843	76050296	562	09-May-2022 19:22:12
10844	16020032	509	09-May-2022 19:22:13
10845	17160063	639	09-May-2022 19:22:13
10846	21030389	411	09-May-2022 19:22:13
10847	21060385	638	09-May-2022 19:22:13
10848	21090182	558	09-May-2022 19:22:13
10849	21130020	560	09-May-2022 19:22:13
10850	21180146	472	09-May-2022 19:22:13

The VCM at Brgy 8, Caloocan City, with Precinct ID: 75010022 printed ER at 21:23:21 of May 09, 2022

Transparency Server Received the ER at 19:24:30 of May 9, 2022

Or 1 hour, 59 minutes, 51 seconds *BEFORE* the ER was printed!

NO.	CLUSTERED	ACTUAL	RECEPTION DATETIME
14251	10210085	561	09-May-2022 19:24:30
14252	10240036	424	09-May-2022 19:24:30
14253	14060046	654	09-May-2022 19:24:30
14254	21080121	619	09-May-2022 19:24:30
14255	21210020	480	09-May-2022 19:24:30
14256	22260241	704	09-May-2022 19:24:30
14257	29140052	366	09-May-2022 19:24:30
14258	29160004	321	09-May-2022 19:24:30
14259	31260016	519	09-May-2022 19:24:30
14260	37050005	575	09-May-2022 19:24:30
14261	37380216	500	09-May-2022 19:24:30
14262	40050042	621	09-May-2022 19:24:30
14263	41070014	472	09-May-2022 19:24:30
14264	46050011	635	09-May-2022 19:24:30
14265	50080004	496	09-May-2022 19:24:30
14266	54130049	646	09-May-2022 19:24:30
14267	55440026	456	09-May-2022 19:24:30
14268	55480007	634	09-May-2022 19:24:30
14269	58040030	631	09-May-2022 19:24:30
14270	58050062	538	09-May-2022 19:24:30
14271	60050015	468	09-May-2022 19:24:30
14272	63060033	643	09-May-2022 19:24:30
14273	63120070	617	09-May-2022 19:24:30
14274	63170018	564	09-May-2022 19:24:30
14275	64180033	368	09-May-2022 19:24:30
14276	74030596	581	09-May-2022 19:24:30
14277	74090125	513	09-May-2022 19:24:30
14278	75010022	386	09-May-2022 19:24:30
14279	03100006	503	09-May-2022 19:24:30
14280	03130029	535	09-May-2022 19:24:31
14281	10140189	664	09-May-2022 19:24:31
14282	10140328	492	09-May-2022 19:24:31

The VCM at Brgy 90, Caloocan City, with Precinct ID: 75010775 printed ER at 19:54:35 of May 09, 2022

Transparency Server Received the ER at 19:21:14 of May 9, 2022

Or 33 minutes, 21 seconds *BEFORE* the ER was printed!

NO.	CLUSTERED	ACTUAL	RECEPTION DATETIME
9251	74040262	463	09-May-2022 19:21:14
9252	75010482	659	09-May-2022 19:21:14
9253	75010775	624	09-May-2022 19:21:14
9254	75010856	675	09-May-2022 19:21:14
9255	75046286	502	09-May-2022 19:21:14
9256	76050126	381	09-May-2022 19:21:14
9257	01230009	480	09-May-2022 19:21:15
9258	05060092	451	09-May-2022 19:21:15
9259	10310053	662	09-May-2022 19:21:15
9260	17330016	299	09-May-2022 19:21:15
9261	21050085	456	09-May-2022 19:21:15
9262	21090089	575	09-May-2022 19:21:15
9263	21110083	560	09-May-2022 19:21:15
9264	22210025	511	09-May-2022 19:21:15
9265	29240037	458	09-May-2022 19:21:15
9266	29250033	563	09-May-2022 19:21:15
9267	31210008	633	09-May-2022 19:21:15
9268	37490003	591	09-May-2022 19:21:15
9269	38170010	308	09-May-2022 19:21:15
9270	39061175	442	09-May-2022 19:21:15
9271	39061615	434	09-May-2022 19:21:15
9272	39141419	310	09-May-2022 19:21:15
9273	49030255	531	09-May-2022 19:21:15
9274	49080114	662	09-May-2022 19:21:15
9275	56470024	491	09-May-2022 19:21:15
9276	58040085	596	09-May-2022 19:21:15

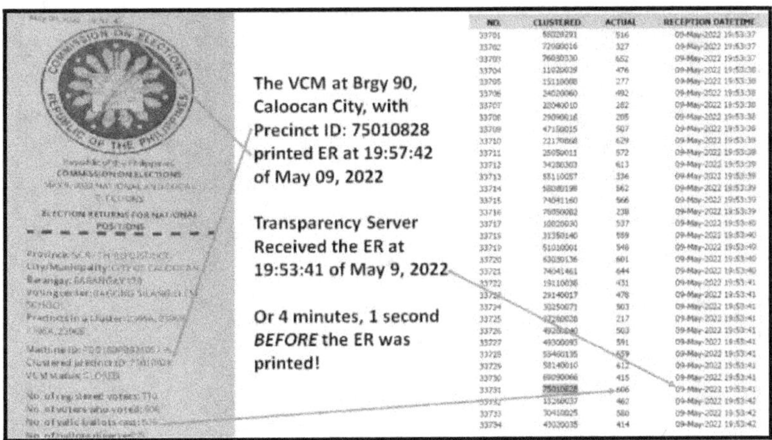

The VCM at Brgy 90, Caloocan City, with Precinct ID: 75010828 printed ER at 19:57:42 of May 09, 2022

Transparency Server Received the ER at 19:53:41 of May 9, 2022

Or 4 minutes, 1 second *BEFORE* the ER was printed!

NO.	CLUSTERED	ACTUAL	RECEPTION DATETIME
33701	58028291	516	09-May-2022 19:53:37
33702	72090016	327	09-May-2022 19:53:37
33703	76030330	652	09-May-2022 19:53:37
33704	11020039	476	09-May-2022 19:53:38
33705	15110008	277	09-May-2022 19:53:38
33706	24020060	492	09-May-2022 19:53:38
33707	28040010	282	09-May-2022 19:53:38
33708	29090016	205	09-May-2022 19:53:38
33709	47150015	507	09-May-2022 19:53:38
33710	22170068	629	09-May-2022 19:53:38
33711	25050011	572	09-May-2022 19:53:38
33712	34280303	613	09-May-2022 19:53:39
33713	55110087	336	09-May-2022 19:53:39
33714	58080198	562	09-May-2022 19:53:39
33715	74041160	566	09-May-2022 19:53:39
33716	76050082	238	09-May-2022 19:53:39
33717	10020030	537	09-May-2022 19:53:40
33718	31350140	559	09-May-2022 19:53:40
33719	51010001	546	09-May-2022 19:53:40
33720	63030136	601	09-May-2022 19:53:40
33721	74041461	644	09-May-2022 19:53:40
33722	19110038	431	09-May-2022 19:53:41
33723	29140017	478	09-May-2022 19:53:41
33724	30250071	503	09-May-2022 19:53:41
33725	42280038	217	09-May-2022 19:53:41
33726	49280040	503	09-May-2022 19:53:41
33727	49300093	591	09-May-2022 19:53:41
33728	55460135	659	09-May-2022 19:53:41
33729	58140010	612	09-May-2022 19:53:41
33730	69090066	415	09-May-2022 19:53:41
33731	75010828	606	09-May-2022 19:53:41
33732	13260037	462	09-May-2022 19:53:42
33733	30410025	580	09-May-2022 19:53:42
33734	43030035	414	09-May-2022 19:53:42

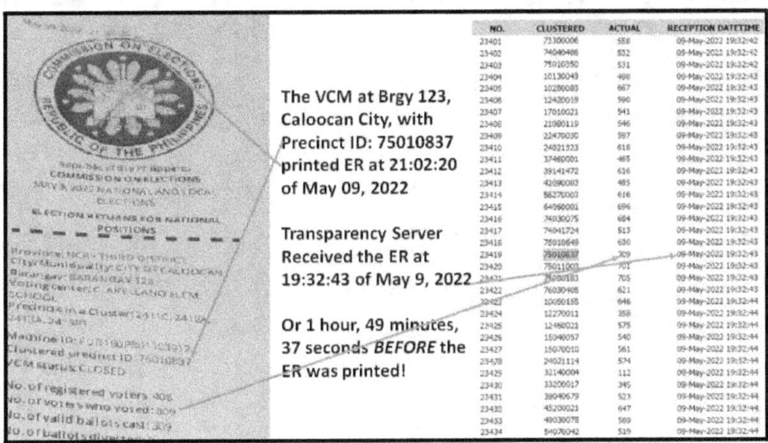

The VCM at Brgy 123, Caloocan City, with Precinct ID: 75010837 printed ER at 21:02:20 of May 09, 2022

Transparency Server Received the ER at 19:32:43 of May 9, 2022

Or 1 hour, 49 minutes, 37 seconds *BEFORE* the ER was printed!

NO.	CLUSTERED	ACTUAL	RECEPTION DATETIME
23401	73300006	558	09-May-2022 19:32:42
23402	74046486	532	09-May-2022 19:32:42
23403	75010350	531	09-May-2022 19:32:42
23404	10130043	498	09-May-2022 19:32:43
23405	10280083	667	09-May-2022 19:32:43
23406	12420019	590	09-May-2022 19:32:43
23407	17010021	541	09-May-2022 19:32:43
23408	21080119	546	09-May-2022 19:32:43
23409	22470030	597	09-May-2022 19:32:43
23410	24021323	618	09-May-2022 19:32:43
23411	37460001	465	09-May-2022 19:32:43
23412	39141472	616	09-May-2022 19:32:43
23413	42090083	485	09-May-2022 19:32:43
23414	56270003	616	09-May-2022 19:32:43
23415	64060001	696	09-May-2022 19:32:43
23416	74030075	684	09-May-2022 19:32:43
23417	74041724	513	09-May-2022 19:32:43
23418	75010649	630	09-May-2022 19:32:43
23419	75010837	309	09-May-2022 19:32:43
23420	75011003	701	09-May-2022 19:32:43
23421	76050183	705	09-May-2022 19:32:43
23422	76030408	621	09-May-2022 19:32:43
23423	10050155	646	09-May-2022 19:32:44
23424	12270011	358	09-May-2022 19:32:44
23425	12480021	575	09-May-2022 19:32:44
23426	15040057	540	09-May-2022 19:32:44
23427	15070010	561	09-May-2022 19:32:44
23428	24021114	574	09-May-2022 19:32:44
23429	32140004	112	09-May-2022 19:32:44
23430	33200017	345	09-May-2022 19:32:44
23431	39040679	523	09-May-2022 19:32:44
23432	45200021	647	09-May-2022 19:32:44
23433	49030075	589	09-May-2022 19:32:44
23434	54070042	519	09-May-2022 19:32:44

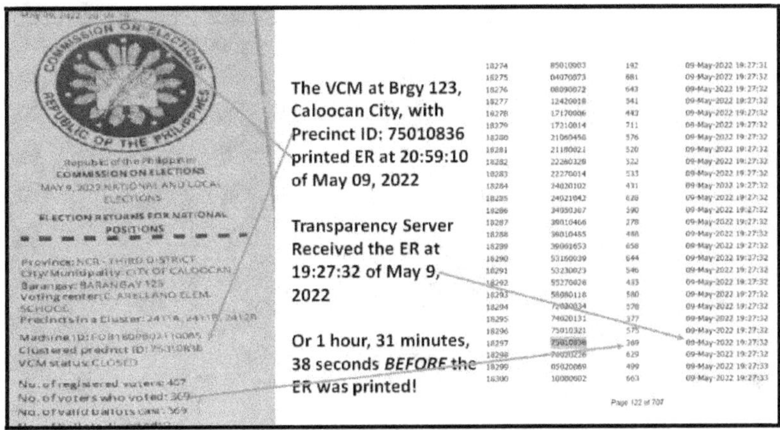

The VCM at Brgy 123, Caloocan City, with Precinct ID: 75010836 printed ER at 20:59:10 of May 09, 2022

Transparency Server Received the ER at 19:27:32 of May 9, 2022

Or 1 hour, 31 minutes, 38 seconds *BEFORE* the ER was printed!

NO.	CLUSTERED	ACTUAL	RECEPTION DATETIME
18274	85010903	192	09-May-2022 19:27:31
18275	04070073	681	09-May-2022 19:27:32
18276	08090072	643	09-May-2022 19:27:32
18277	12420018	341	09-May-2022 19:27:32
18278	17170006	443	09-May-2022 19:27:32
18279	17210014	711	09-May-2022 19:27:32
18280	21060458	576	09-May-2022 19:27:32
18281	21180021	520	09-May-2022 19:27:32
18282	22280328	322	09-May-2022 19:27:32
18283	22270014	513	09-May-2022 19:27:32
18284	34020102	431	09-May-2022 19:27:32
18285	24021042	628	09-May-2022 19:27:32
18286	34050307	590	09-May-2022 19:27:32
18287	39010466	278	09-May-2022 19:27:32
18288	39010485	488	09-May-2022 19:27:32
18289	39061653	658	09-May-2022 19:27:32
18290	53160039	644	09-May-2022 19:27:32
18291	53230023	546	09-May-2022 19:27:32
18292	55270028	433	09-May-2022 19:27:32
18293	58080118	580	09-May-2022 19:27:32
18294	72030034	570	09-May-2022 19:27:32
18295	74020131	377	09-May-2022 19:27:32
18296	75010321	575	09-May-2022 19:27:32
18297	75010836	309	09-May-2022 19:27:32
18298	76020226	629	09-May-2022 19:27:32
18299	05020069	499	09-May-2022 19:27:33
18300	10080002	663	09-May-2022 19:27:33

Page 122 of 707

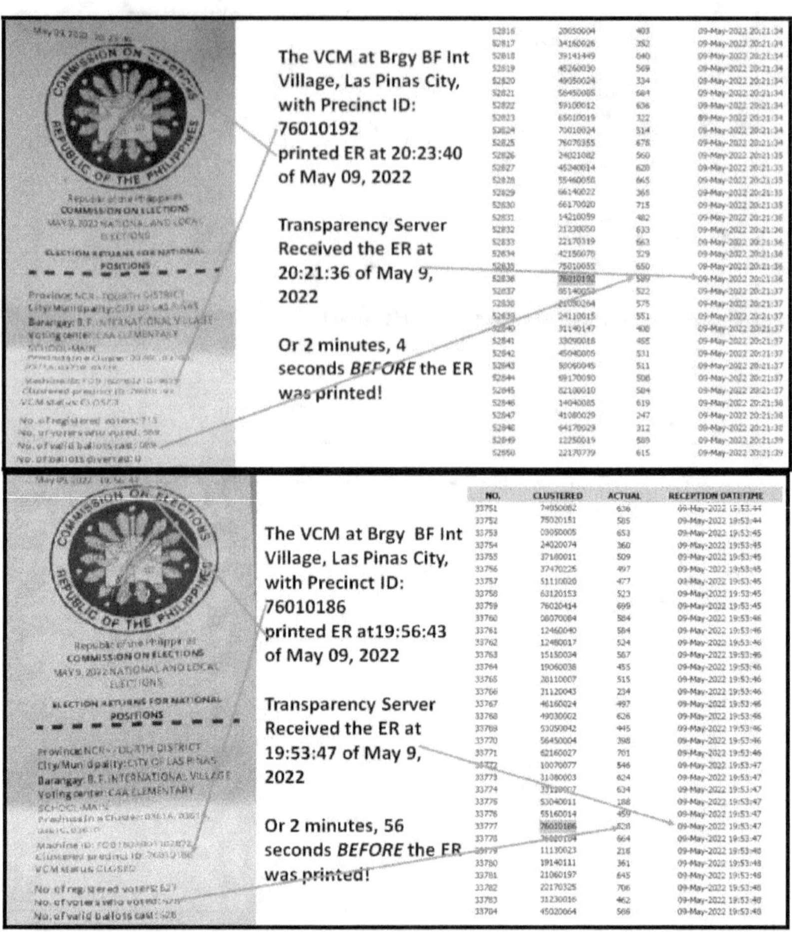

Section 1

The VCM at Brgy BF Int Village, Las Pinas City, with Precinct ID: 76010192 printed ER at 20:23:40 of May 09, 2022

Transparency Server Received the ER at 20:21:36 of May 9, 2022

Or 2 minutes, 4 seconds *BEFORE* the ER was printed!

NO.	CLUSTERED	ACTUAL	RECEPTION DATETIME
52816	20050004	403	09-May-2022 20:21:34
52817	34160026	382	09-May-2022 20:21:34
52818	39141449	640	09-May-2022 20:21:34
52819	45260030	569	09-May-2022 20:21:34
52820	49050024	334	09-May-2022 20:21:34
52821	56450085	684	09-May-2022 20:21:34
52822	59100012	636	09-May-2022 20:21:34
52823	65010019	322	09-May-2022 20:21:34
52824	70010024	514	09-May-2022 20:21:34
52825	76070355	678	09-May-2022 20:21:34
52826	24021082	560	09-May-2022 20:21:35
52827	45240014	620	09-May-2022 20:21:35
52828	55460058	665	09-May-2022 20:21:35
52829	66140022	365	09-May-2022 20:21:35
52830	66170020	715	09-May-2022 20:21:35
52831	14210059	482	09-May-2022 20:21:36
52832	21230050	633	09-May-2022 20:21:36
52833	22170319	663	09-May-2022 20:21:36
52834	42150070	329	09-May-2022 20:21:36
52835	75010055	650	09-May-2022 20:21:36
52836	76010192	589	09-May-2022 20:21:36
52837	85140058	522	09-May-2022 20:21:37
52838	61080264	575	09-May-2022 20:21:37
52839	24110015	551	09-May-2022 20:21:37
52840	31140147	400	09-May-2022 20:21:37
52841	33090018	485	09-May-2022 20:21:37
52842	45040006	531	09-May-2022 20:21:37
52843	50060045	511	09-May-2022 20:21:37
52844	69170090	506	09-May-2022 20:21:37
52845	82100010	504	09-May-2022 20:21:37
52846	14040085	619	09-May-2022 20:21:38
52847	41080029	247	09-May-2022 20:21:38
52848	64170029	312	09-May-2022 20:21:38
52849	12250019	589	09-May-2022 20:21:39
52850	22170779	615	09-May-2022 20:21:39

Section 2

The VCM at Brgy BF Int Village, Las Pinas City, with Precinct ID: 76010186 printed ER at 19:56:43 of May 09, 2022

Transparency Server Received the ER at 19:53:47 of May 9, 2022

Or 2 minutes, 56 seconds *BEFORE* the ER was printed!

NO.	CLUSTERED	ACTUAL	RECEPTION DATETIME
33751	74050062	636	09-May-2022 19:53:44
33752	75020151	585	09-May-2022 19:53:44
33753	09050005	653	09-May-2022 19:53:45
33754	24020074	360	09-May-2022 19:53:45
33755	37180011	509	09-May-2022 19:53:45
33756	37470225	497	09-May-2022 19:53:45
33757	51110020	477	09-May-2022 19:53:45
33758	63120153	523	09-May-2022 19:53:45
33759	76020414	699	09-May-2022 19:53:45
33760	08070004	584	09-May-2022 19:53:46
33761	12460040	584	09-May-2022 19:53:46
33762	12480017	524	09-May-2022 19:53:46
33763	15150034	567	09-May-2022 19:53:46
33764	19060038	455	09-May-2022 19:53:46
33765	28110007	515	09-May-2022 19:53:46
33766	21120043	234	09-May-2022 19:53:46
33767	46160024	497	09-May-2022 19:53:46
33768	49030002	626	09-May-2022 19:53:46
33769	53050042	445	09-May-2022 19:53:46
33770	56450004	398	09-May-2022 19:53:46
33771	62160027	701	09-May-2022 19:53:46
33772	10070077	546	09-May-2022 19:53:47
33773	31080003	624	09-May-2022 19:53:47
33774	33120002	634	09-May-2022 19:53:47
33775	53040011	188	09-May-2022 19:53:47
33776	55160014	459	09-May-2022 19:53:47
33777	76010186	528	09-May-2022 19:53:47
33778	76080104	664	09-May-2022 19:53:47
33779	11130023	218	09-May-2022 19:53:48
33780	19140111	361	09-May-2022 19:53:48
33781	21060197	645	09-May-2022 19:53:48
33782	22170325	706	09-May-2022 19:53:48
33783	31230016	462	09-May-2022 19:53:48
33784	45020064	566	09-May-2022 19:53:48

Section 3

The VCM at Brgy Talon Dos, Las Pinas City, with Precinct ID: 76010259 printed ER at 20:04:59 of May 09, 2022

Transparency Server Received the ER at 20:00:50 of May 9, 2022

Or 4 minutes, 9 seconds *BEFORE* the ER was printed!

NO.	CLUSTERED	ACTUAL	RECEPTION DATETIME
38551	47060011	339	09-May-2022 20:00:50
38552	98100030	536	09-May-2022 20:00:50
38553	60070003	392	09-May-2022 20:00:50
38554	68170043	500	09-May-2022 20:00:50
38555	73080060	424	09-May-2022 20:00:50
38556	76010160	622	09-May-2022 20:00:50
38557	76010259	587	09-May-2022 20:00:50
38558	90030027	982	09-May-2022 20:00:50
38559	10090032	688	09-May-2022 20:00:51
38560	13070023	370	09-May-2022 20:00:51
38561	13140018	417	09-May-2022 20:00:51
38562	53080005	110	09-May-2022 20:00:51
38563	53160058	435	09-May-2022 20:00:51
38564	54100060	546	09-May-2022 20:00:51
38565	56180033	348	09-May-2022 20:00:51
38566	62020013	357	09-May-2022 20:00:51
38567	66020061	434	09-May-2022 20:00:51
38568	71120032	321	09-May-2022 20:00:51
38569	73380007	635	09-May-2022 20:00:51
38570	74010290	595	09-May-2022 20:00:51
38571	77030003	662	09-May-2022 20:00:51
38572	80070023	395	09-May-2022 20:00:51
38573	08110007	492	09-May-2022 20:00:52
38574	08110033	526	09-May-2022 20:00:52
38575	12230029	602	09-May-2022 20:00:52
38576	17240004	659	09-May-2022 20:00:52
38577	25100013	359	09-May-2022 20:00:52
38578	34020054	504	09-May-2022 20:00:52
38579	75040098	500	09-May-2022 20:00:52
38580	39010609	416	09-May-2022 20:00:52
38581	47090017	457	09-May-2022 20:00:52
38582	52120022	416	09-May-2022 20:00:52
38583	75020246	579	09-May-2022 20:00:52
38584	76010095	611	09-May-2022 20:00:52

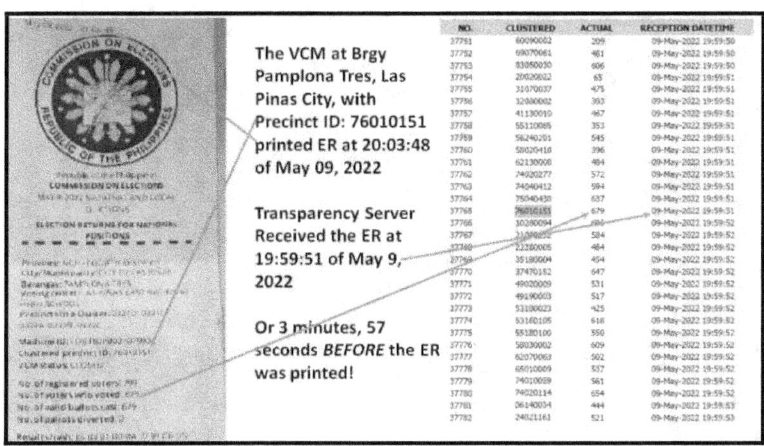

The VCM at Brgy Pamplona Tres, Las Pinas City, with Precinct ID: 76010151 printed ER at 20:03:48 of May 09, 2022

Transparency Server Received the ER at 19:59:51 of May 9, 2022

Or 3 minutes, 57 seconds *BEFORE* the ER was printed!

NO.	CLUSTERED	ACTUAL	RECEPTION DATETIME
37751	60090062	209	09-May-2022 19:59:50
37752	69070061	461	09-May-2022 19:59:50
37753	83050030	606	09-May-2022 19:59:50
37754	20020012	65	09-May-2022 19:59:51
37755	31070037	475	09-May-2022 19:59:51
37756	32080002	393	09-May-2022 19:59:51
37757	41130010	467	09-May-2022 19:59:51
37758	55110085	353	09-May-2022 19:59:51
37759	56240201	545	09-May-2022 19:59:51
37760	58020418	396	09-May-2022 19:59:51
37761	62130008	484	09-May-2022 19:59:51
37762	74020277	572	09-May-2022 19:59:51
37763	74040412	594	09-May-2022 19:59:51
37764	75040430	637	09-May-2022 19:59:51
37765	76010151	679	09-May-2022 19:59:51
37766	10280094	686	09-May-2022 19:59:52
37767	21090052	584	09-May-2022 19:59:52
37768	22280005	464	09-May-2022 19:59:52
37769	35180004	454	09-May-2022 19:59:52
37770	37470152	647	09-May-2022 19:59:52
37771	49020009	531	09-May-2022 19:59:52
37772	49190003	517	09-May-2022 19:59:52
37773	53100023	425	09-May-2022 19:59:52
37774	53160105	618	09-May-2022 19:59:52
37775	55180100	550	09-May-2022 19:59:52
37776	58030002	609	09-May-2022 19:59:52
37777	62070063	502	09-May-2022 19:59:52
37778	65010009	537	09-May-2022 19:59:52
37779	74010059	561	09-May-2022 19:59:52
37780	74020114	654	09-May-2022 19:59:52
37781	06140034	444	09-May-2022 19:59:53
37782	24021161	521	09-May-2022 19:59:53

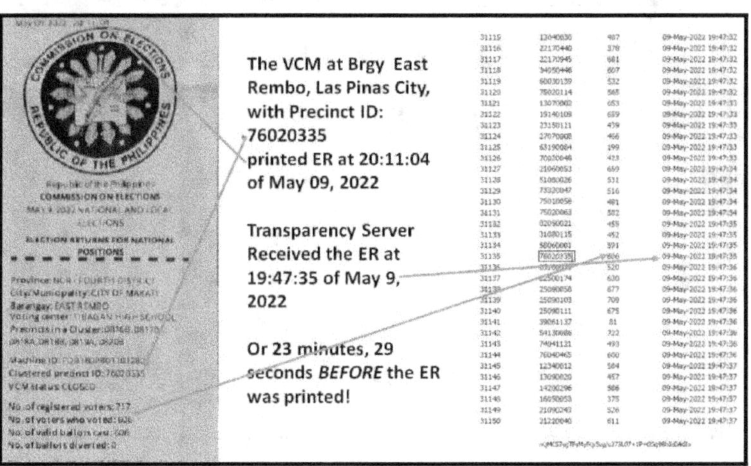

The VCM at Brgy East Rembo, Las Pinas City, with Precinct ID: 76020335 printed ER at 20:11:04 of May 09, 2022

Transparency Server Received the ER at 19:47:35 of May 9, 2022

Or 23 minutes, 29 seconds *BEFORE* the ER was printed!

NO.	CLUSTERED	ACTUAL	RECEPTION DATETIME
31115	13040830	487	09-May-2022 19:47:32
31116	22170440	378	09-May-2022 19:47:32
31117	22170945	681	09-May-2022 19:47:32
31118	34050446	607	09-May-2022 19:47:32
31119	60030139	532	09-May-2022 19:47:32
31120	75020114	565	09-May-2022 19:47:32
31121	13070002	653	09-May-2022 19:47:33
31122	19140109	689	09-May-2022 19:47:33
31123	23150111	439	09-May-2022 19:47:33
31124	27070908	466	09-May-2022 19:47:33
31125	63190084	199	09-May-2022 19:47:33
31126	70070046	423	09-May-2022 19:47:33
31127	21060053	669	09-May-2022 19:47:34
31128	51080026	531	09-May-2022 19:47:34
31129	73320047	516	09-May-2022 19:47:34
31130	75010058	481	09-May-2022 19:47:34
31131	75020063	582	09-May-2022 19:47:34
31132	02090021	459	09-May-2022 19:47:35
31133	31080115	452	09-May-2022 19:47:35
31134	58060001	591	09-May-2022 19:47:35
31135	76020335	606	09-May-2022 19:47:35
31136	03090030	520	09-May-2022 19:47:36
31137	22500174	630	09-May-2022 19:47:36
31138	25090058	677	09-May-2022 19:47:36
31139	25090103	709	09-May-2022 19:47:36
31140	25090111	675	09-May-2022 19:47:36
31141	39061137	81	09-May-2022 19:47:36
31142	54130686	722	09-May-2022 19:47:36
31143	74041121	493	09-May-2022 19:47:36
31144	76040465	600	09-May-2022 19:47:36
31145	12340012	584	09-May-2022 19:47:37
31146	13090020	457	09-May-2022 19:47:37
31147	14290296	586	09-May-2022 19:47:37
31148	16050053	375	09-May-2022 19:47:37
31149	21090243	526	09-May-2022 19:47:37
31150	21220040	611	09-May-2022 19:47:37

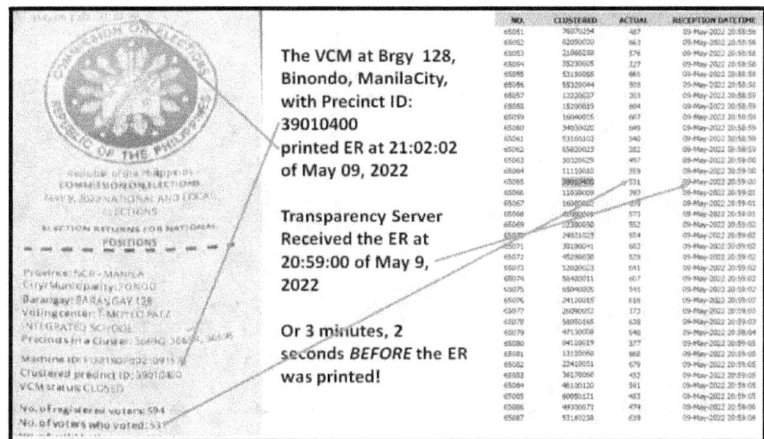

The VCM at Brgy 128, Binondo, ManilaCity, with Precinct ID: 39010400 printed ER at 21:02:02 of May 09, 2022

Transparency Server Received the ER at 20:59:00 of May 9, 2022

Or 3 minutes, 2 seconds *BEFORE* the ER was printed!

NO.	CLUSTERED	ACTUAL	RECEPTION DATETIME
65051	76070254	467	09-May-2022 20:58:58
65052	82050020	863	09-May-2022 20:58:58
65053	21060288	576	09-May-2022 20:58:58
65054	35230605	327	09-May-2022 20:58:58
65055	53190068	665	09-May-2022 20:58:58
65056	55320044	505	09-May-2022 20:58:58
65057	12220037	263	09-May-2022 20:58:59
65058	15200019	604	09-May-2022 20:58:59
65059	16040005	667	09-May-2022 20:58:59
65060	34030020	649	09-May-2022 20:58:59
65061	53160102	540	09-May-2022 20:58:59
65062	65030023	282	09-May-2022 20:58:59
65063	90320029	497	09-May-2022 20:59:00
65064	11110010	369	09-May-2022 20:59:00
65065	39010400	531	09-May-2022 20:59:00
65066	11030009	780	09-May-2022 20:59:01
65067	16080002	609	09-May-2022 20:59:01
65068	40090069	571	09-May-2022 20:59:01
65069	22380030	552	09-May-2022 20:59:02
65070	24021023	554	09-May-2022 20:59:02
65071	30190041	662	09-May-2022 20:59:02
65072	45290030	529	09-May-2022 20:59:02
65073	52020023	641	09-May-2022 20:59:02
65074	56400011	607	09-May-2022 20:59:02
65075	65040005	545	09-May-2022 20:59:02
65076	24120015	616	09-May-2022 20:59:03
65077	26090052	173	09-May-2022 20:59:03
65078	58050165	638	09-May-2022 20:59:03
65079	47130058	540	09-May-2022 20:59:04
65080	64110019	377	09-May-2022 20:59:05
65081	13130060	968	09-May-2022 20:59:05
65082	22410051	679	09-May-2022 20:59:05
65083	36170068	432	09-May-2022 20:59:05
65084	46100120	591	09-May-2022 20:59:05
65085	60050121	483	09-May-2022 20:59:05
65086	49300071	474	09-May-2022 20:59:06
65087	53180238	639	09-May-2022 20:59:06

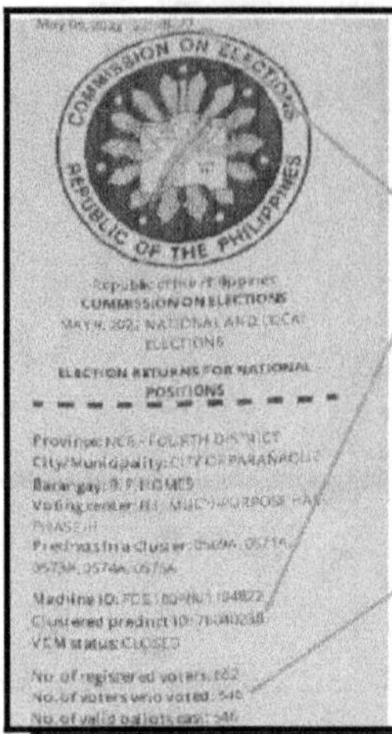

The VCM at Brgy BF Homes, Paranaque City, with Precinct ID: 76040238 printed ER at 22:28:33 of May 09, 2022

Transparency Server Received the ER at 22:24:02 of May 9, 2022

Or 4 minutes, 31 seconds *BEFORE* the ER was printed!

NO.	CLUSTERED	ACTUAL	RECEPTION DATETIME
78551	46130010	601	09-May-2022 22:24:00
78552	48180018	543	09-May-2022 22:24:00
78553	62070030	138	09-May-2022 22:24:00
78554	63060165	637	09-May-2022 22:24:00
78555	66240011	483	09-May-2022 22:24:02
78556	76040238	546	09-May-2022 22:24:02
78557	48060029	280	09-May-2022 22:24:03
78558	56030033	496	09-May-2022 22:24:03
78559	35040308	672	09-May-2022 22:24:04
78560	30029048	384	09-May-2022 22:24:04
78561	48020024	441	09-May-2022 22:24:04
78562	56230039	468	09-May-2022 22:24:04
78563	30010051	545	09-May-2022 22:24:05
78564	43220009	479	09-May-2022 22:24:05
78565	47080055	480	09-May-2022 22:24:05
78566	33110010	536	09-May-2022 22:24:06
78567	50010005	354	09-May-2022 22:24:06
78568	60010023	149	09-May-2022 22:24:07
78569	12440016	685	09-May-2022 22:24:08
78570	19030005	480	09-May-2022 22:24:08
78571	45090086	667	09-May-2022 22:24:08
78572	45010436	705	09-May-2022 22:24:10
78573	56220031	526	09-May-2022 22:24:10
78574	77040016	479	09-May-2022 22:24:10
78575	66160016	363	09-May-2022 22:24:11
78576	99150019	447	09-May-2022 22:24:12
78577	64140019	449	09-May-2022 22:24:12
78578	43240023	520	09-May-2022 22:24:13
78579	72230003	617	09-May-2022 22:24:13
78580	54050094	653	09-May-2022 22:24:14
78581	37100025	149	09-May-2022 22:24:15
78582	56240116	671	09-May-2022 22:24:15
78583	02010047	997	09-May-2022 22:24:16
78584	30070050	413	09-May-2022 22:24:16
78585	53120027	541	09-May-2022 22:24:16
78586	54060012	473	09-May-2022 22:24:16
78587	82030028	568	09-May-2022 22:24:16

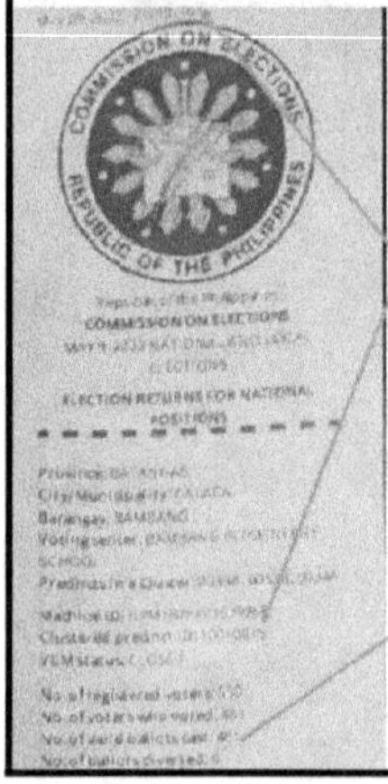

The VCM at Brgy Bambang, Batangas City, with Precinct ID: 10070015 printed ER at 21:10:16 of May 09, 2022

Transparency Server Received the ER at 19:25:01 of May 9, 2022

Or 1 hour, 45 minutes, 15 seconds *BEFORE* the ER was printed!

NO.	CLUSTERED	ACTUAL	RECEPTION DATETIME
14951	73320508	550	09-May-2022 19:25:00
14952	74040204	559	09-May-2022 19:25:00
14953	75010265	466	09-May-2022 19:25:00
14954	82050016	582	09-May-2022 19:25:00
14955	83050035	510	09-May-2022 19:25:00
14956	10070015	481	09-May-2022 19:25:01
14957	10220013	568	09-May-2022 19:25:01
14958	14040041	546	09-May-2022 19:25:01
14959	20040035	504	09-May-2022 19:25:01
14960	21030153	582	09-May-2022 19:25:01
14961	21060047	594	09-May-2022 19:25:01
14962	21060072	509	09-May-2022 19:25:01
14963	21090290	624	09-May-2022 19:25:01
14964	21140033	488	09-May-2022 19:25:01
14965	21200029	430	09-May-2022 19:25:01
14966	22420027	513	09-May-2022 19:25:01
14967	24020288	593	09-May-2022 19:25:01
14968	29240048	425	09-May-2022 19:25:01
14969	46040014	470	09-May-2022 19:25:01
14970	47170003	588	09-May-2022 19:25:01
14971	54130096	532	09-May-2022 19:25:01
14972	63030142	497	09-May-2022 19:25:01
14973	71010006	475	09-May-2022 19:25:01
14974	71070118	492	09-May-2022 19:25:01
14975	73320210	562	09-May-2022 19:25:01
14976	74010178	627	09-May-2022 19:25:01
14977	74020254	607	09-May-2022 19:25:01
14978	74041014	614	09-May-2022 19:25:01
14979	75010227	575	09-May-2022 19:25:01
14980	75040092	583	09-May-2022 19:25:01
14981	76020450	662	09-May-2022 19:25:01
14982	81020012	626	09-May-2022 19:25:01
14983	21060399	581	09-May-2022 19:25:02

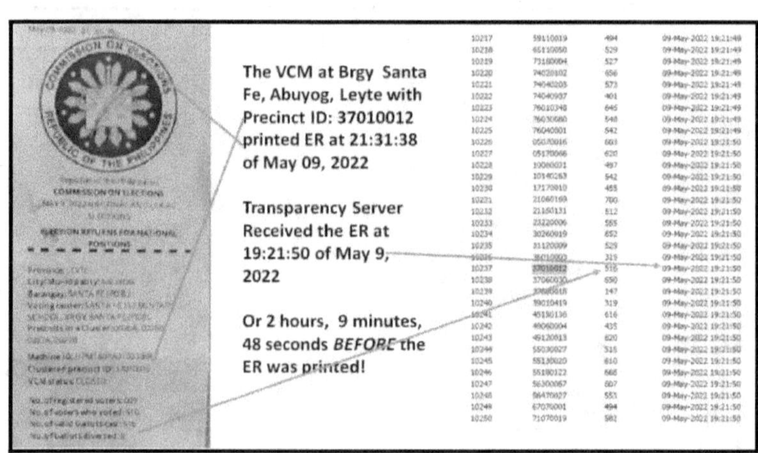

The VCM at Brgy Santa Fe, Abuyog, Leyte with Precinct ID: 37010012 printed ER at 21:31:38 of May 09, 2022

Transparency Server Received the ER at 19:21:50 of May 9, 2022

Or 2 hours, 9 minutes, 48 seconds *BEFORE* the ER was printed!

NO.	CLUSTERED	ACTUAL	RECEPTION DATETIME
10217	59110019	494	09-May-2022 19:21:49
10218	65110050	529	09-May-2022 19:21:49
10219	73180004	527	09-May-2022 19:21:49
10220	74020102	656	09-May-2022 19:21:49
10221	74040205	573	09-May-2022 19:21:49
10222	74040907	401	09-May-2022 19:21:49
10223	76010348	645	09-May-2022 19:21:49
10224	76030680	548	09-May-2022 19:21:49
10225	76040001	542	09-May-2022 19:21:49
10226	05070016	663	09-May-2022 19:21:50
10227	05170066	620	09-May-2022 19:21:50
10228	10060031	497	09-May-2022 19:21:50
10229	10140263	542	09-May-2022 19:21:50
10230	17170010	455	09-May-2022 19:21:50
10231	21060169	700	09-May-2022 19:21:50
10232	21160131	812	09-May-2022 19:21:50
10233	23220006	585	09-May-2022 19:21:50
10234	30260019	652	09-May-2022 19:21:50
10235	31120009	529	09-May-2022 19:21:50
10236	36010002	319	09-May-2022 19:21:50
10237	37010012	518	09-May-2022 19:21:50
10238	37060010	650	09-May-2022 19:21:50
10239	37060018	147	09-May-2022 19:21:50
10240	39010419	319	09-May-2022 19:21:50
10241	45130136	616	09-May-2022 19:21:50
10242	49060004	435	09-May-2022 19:21:50
10243	49120013	620	09-May-2022 19:21:50
10244	55030027	315	09-May-2022 19:21:50
10245	55130020	610	09-May-2022 19:21:50
10246	55180122	666	09-May-2022 19:21:50
10247	56300067	607	09-May-2022 19:21:50
10248	56470027	551	09-May-2022 19:21:50
10249	67070001	494	09-May-2022 19:21:50
10250	71070019	581	09-May-2022 19:21:50

Republic of the Philippines
COMMISSION ON ELECTIONS
MAY 9 2022 NATIONAL AND LOCAL ELECTIONS

ELECTION RETURNS FOR NATIONAL POSITIONS

Province: NCR (THIRD DISTRICT)
City/Municipality: CITY OF VALENZUELA
Barangay: PASO DE BLAS
Voting center: PASO DE BLAS NATIONAL HIGH SCHOOL
Precincts in a Cluster: [illegible]
VCM Status: [illegible]
No. of registered voters: [illegible]
No. of voters who voted: [illegible]
No. of valid ballots cast: [illegible]
No. of ballots ejected: 0

The VCM at Brgy Paso De Blas, Valenzuela City, with Precinct ID: 75040563 printed ER at 21:34:00 of May 09, 2022

Transparency Server Received the ER at 20:16:59 of May 9, 2022

Or 1 hour, 17 minutes, 10 seconds *BEFORE* the ER was printed!

50270	49080079	609	09-May-2022 20:16:57
50271	49250031	590	09-May-2022 20:16:57
50272	56380014	612	09-May-2022 20:16:57
50273	69070058	573	09-May-2022 20:16:57
50274	73320265	576	09-May-2022 20:16:57
50275	15170037	546	09-May-2022 20:16:58
50276	23150037	442	09-May-2022 20:16:58
50277	37050018	516	09-May-2022 20:16:58
50278	37350002	360	09-May-2022 20:16:58
50279	55420012	639	09-May-2022 20:16:58
50280	83040016	501	09-May-2022 20:16:58
50281	08070082	596	09-May-2022 20:16:59
50282	10230090	602	09-May-2022 20:16:59
50283	10280152	609	09-May-2022 20:16:59
50284	19140044	655	09-May-2022 20:16:59
50285	21060266	647	09-May-2022 20:16:59
50286	21230081	572	09-May-2022 20:16:59
50287	22170943	682	09-May-2022 20:16:59
50288	30350011	609	09-May-2022 20:16:59
50289	47100017	505	09-May-2022 20:16:59
50290	52010031	323	09-May-2022 20:16:59
50291	72050029	570	09-May-2022 20:16:59
50292	74050119	607	09-May-2022 20:16:59
50293	75040563	633	09-May-2022 20:16:59
50294	06420014	552	09-May-2022 20:17:00
50295	05110001	670	09-May-2022 20:17:00
50296	13210018	553	09-May-2022 20:17:00
50297	29030011	656	09-May-2022 20:17:00
50298	30220049	316	09-May-2022 20:17:00
50299	34170023	286	09-May-2022 20:17:00

LIST OF VCM RECEIVED MAY 9, 2022 NLE

NO.	CLUSTERED	ACTUAL	RECEPTION DATETIME
105951	39141532	393	11-May-2022 15:54:40
105952	39141533	418	11-May-2022 15:56:44
105953	39141504	482	11-May-2022 15:58:43
105954	36070018	439	11-May-2022 13:59:52
105955	39101368	278	11-May-2022 16:01:25
105956	92120282	0	11-May-2022 16:02:27
105957	39141511	453	11-May-2022 16:03:15
105958	36070006	655	11-May-2022 16:18:21
105959	36070014	3	11-May-2022 16:32:21
105960	92120253	1,000	11-May-2022 17:19:39
105961	92120230	1,000	11-May-2022 17:21:34
105962	92120232	1,000	11-May-2022 17:23:09
105963	92120275	0	11-May-2022 17:24:27
105964	66120038	3	11-May-2022 17:44:51
105965	36120032	324	11-May-2022 17:58:26
105966	38100034	528	11-May-2022 18:01:45
105967	38280033	445	11-May-2022 18:09:22
105968	07010125	434	11-May-2022 18:17:12
105969	36070024	159	11-May-2022 19:16:19
105970	91050015	671	11-May-2022 21:41:37
105971	91050017	588	11-May-2022 21:46:12
105972	91050016	568	11-May-2022 21:48:55
105973	36070001	742	11-May-2022 21:51:07
105974	91050019	606	11-May-2022 21:51:30
105975	91050020	641	11-May-2022 21:53:27
105976	91050021	583	11-May-2022 21:55:59
105977	91050022	614	11-May-2022 21:58:53
105978	91050023	658	11-May-2022 22:00:54
105979	91050024	604	11-May-2022 22:03:07
105980	36120023	248	11-May-2022 22:04:21
105981	91050025	594	13-May-2022 22:05:00
105982	91050016	659	11-May-2022 22:07:18
105983	91050026	606	11-May-2022 22:09:40

NO.	CLUSTERED	ACTUAL	RECEPTION DATETIME
106001	36070019	388	12-May-2022 01:27:27
106002	36310001	532	12-May-2022 01:34:52
106003	36070002	645	12-May-2022 11:01:15
106004	36070023	515	12-May-2022 13:10:11
106005	36070003	542	12-May-2022 14:25:27
106006	36070009	522	12-May-2022 14:36:26
106007	36070005	119	12-May-2022 16:43:27
106008	36050015	341	12-May-2022 23:05:27
106009	36280009	422	24-May-2022 19:22:08
106010	36280003	251	24-May-2022 20:19:52
106011	36280024	181	24-May-2022 20:43:03
106012	36280017	334	24-May-2022 21:07:09
106013	36280006	274	24-May-2022 21:09:38
106014	36280019	265	24-May-2022 21:11:43
106015	36280020	201	24-May-2022 21:19:43
106016	36280001	366	24-May-2022 21:46:07
106017	36280013	247	24-May-2022 21:50:30
106018	36280016	176	24-May-2022 22:21:12
106019	36280015	221	24-May-2022 23:15:04
106020	36280022	191	25-May-2022 01:17:12
106021	36280011	209	25-May-2022 01:17:19
106022	36280018	244	25-May-2022 01:18:43
106023	36280002	244	25-May-2022 03:23:35

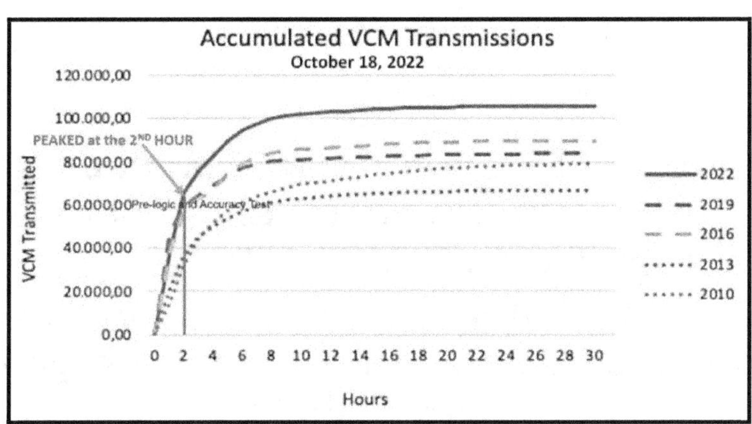

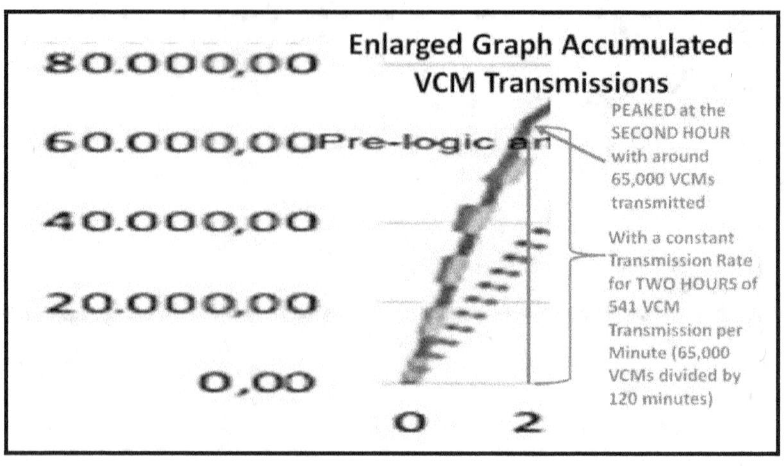

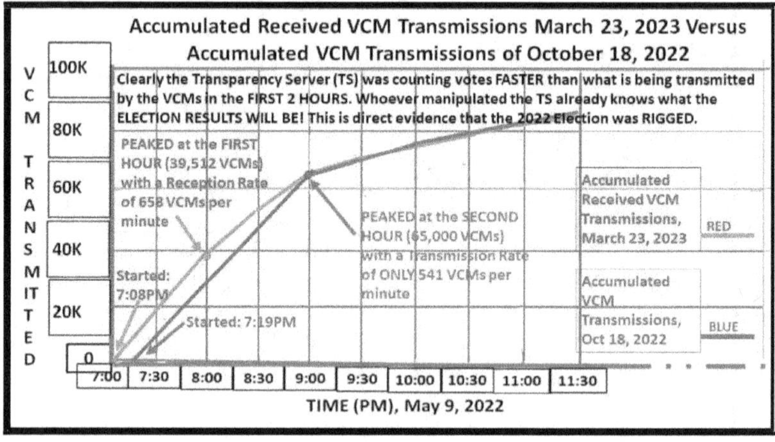

. . . .

13
Shocking Election Results Immediately within2 hours after closing of the elections in May 9, 2022. – I remembered it vividely – Franklin Ysaaac – posted by Tina A. Astorga – May 8, 2023

After months of campaigning, October 21 till May 22, my family and I woke up to line up and cast our final word on who we want to be our next President and VP.

The long wait as thousands showed up as early as 5 am in our precinct was the longest wait just to cast our precious and well guarded ballot . It took us hours even with elderly people who came early .

The tremendous outpouring of voters wearing the color of our favorite candidate outnumbered the few voters who were wearing the other unpopular color . In fact, these unpopular voters were being booed.

Sweating under the heat of the morning and afternoon sun, we managed to finish our acts before sundown .

And early evening hours at around 7, I got calls from my siblings in US telling me it's game over as the unpopular candidate has already won in the millions . The US networks were already reporting the election was over even if there were still long lines of voters outside many precincts in my district.

My kids couldn't believe if this was true. We switched on to local channels and exactly what these US networks were announcing was also the same as these networks picked them up from local networks.

My kids cried and asked me how that was possible if all the precincts have not been reporting the usual early returns from precincts around the country .

I was too dumbfounded to answer their questions and I couldn't believe what was happening .

I called several friends from nearby towns and they gave me the same answer.

It seemed that the survey results matched the early results .

I wasn't relying on these surveys from the very beginning as I was relying more on Google trends which accurately predicted the results from elections in other countries.

Even after the closing of election hour, Google trends was still forecasting the true winner .

Was there an error or factor that Google trends didn't account for on making the prediction.

I asked my co IT friends and they said the Google trends is very reliable as it is based on social media numbers .

I couldn't get enough sleep as I was praying that in the next few hours the results would change.

The time stopped at around 8 pm and I knew that with millions counted already in favor of the unpopular candidate, the favorite cannot overcome those numbers.

I was then challenged by my family and siblings to check and double check if this was authentic.

I know little about election process but since this was an automated election system I began to investigate how an electronic system can alter or probably change direction if the masses were voting for the favorite candidate and the results went to the unpopular candidate.

If the mass of campaigners during the many rallies I joined were to be followed, it's next to impossible to see the voters changing their minds overnite on who to vote for.

A few days after the fateful May 9, I began to ask questions to myself and I posted my queries in my Fb account . I received few likes because my Fb was private and I have very few friends. Some of my friends encouraged me to go public so more people can read my views and queries .

When I went public days after, my Fb was swarmed by a good number who liked my posts and who wanted to be my friends . I responded that I was not prepared to accept many friends as I am really a very private person. They replied by just following my posts.

It was then that after recalling what I was writing about my questions on the election results, my suspicions were becoming obvious .

I was reading what other commentaries were writing about but I was more focused on the election system that if the system were fully automated, then the results could not be changed and if the sentiment of voters which was known in real surveys and campaign rallies, then an automated system cannot change the results unless the system was hacked or manipulated .

My daily posts inquiring about the process which I learned like the VCM, the SD cards, the Ers, telcos and transmission logs came to the front line as I busy connecting the dots. I mentioned in one of my posts that if the system was seamless or straight through processing, then there is no problem in accepting the results .

But the results were confounding and I didn't believe that the system was seamless and somebody must have done something to alter the system .

Weeks and months after I began publishing in my posts about the incredulous results, I got calls from my friends here and abroad and I was already being interviewed about how I was making my judgement or conclusions.

I won't go over the subsequent months of how the TNTrio became a reality as I have already written about how we started this campaign for truth about the election.

If I were to go back to my conclusion then and what we have uncovered lately, my suspicions or queries were proven to be correct .

This is the conclusion based on my own observations last year .

" the automated system was not a straight through processing or what we in IT call STP. If the system was seamless, then the results would have been correct . But the system was broken Frand it looked like the front end part didn't end up in the back end part. This means the casting and counting may be real but it stopped there. The end part which is the transparency server was running independent of the front end part leading me to believe somebody was manufacturing the end part "

I discussed this with my IT staff and they claimed they can also manufacture the end part as there was no connection between the front end and the back end .

I remember one client who wanted an integrated system but who wanted me to stop at the accounting part as he wanted to massage the taxable amount as he didn't want to pay rhe correct taxes . I turned it down because if BIR checked out my system and if my system will be found to be corrupted then I would be liable too.

I turned down the offer and it cost me a fortune for not accepting the request of my client . That client is now in deep trouble with BIR and I withdrew and deleted my system from his computers .

This campaign for truth is not yet over as the guilty parties still want to defend their weak positions.

Maybe they want thunder and lighting to befall on them after we end our 9th day of novena today .

Please join us in our novena at the Manila cathedral where Stella Maris sisters will lead the rosary, litany and novena.

St Joseph, pray for us.

Mama Mary, pray for us.

Our Lord Jesus, please keep us strong in our faith in you and defend the rights and fight of Filipinos for truth and transparency in our election.

Amen .

....

14
THE PEOPLE MANDAMUS IS A PEOPLE'S ACT OF CITIZENSHIP: CALLING THE OPPOSITION TO LEAD THE PEOPLE MANDAMUS –

Tina A. Astorga

The People Mandamus is different from an electoral protest of any one particular candidate. It is the Filipino people compelling Comelec to be transparent & truthful about the elections. They should make public the transparency logs for public scrutiny to dispel any iota of doubt about the integrity of elections 2022. Signing the People's Mandamus is an act of citizenship of every Filipino who has a right to the sanctity of his or her vote.

Since the current leadership has profited from the rigging of the elections based on direct evidence of fraud, they understandably would want to keep the status quo. It is thus incumbent on the Opposition to lead the signing of the People Mandamus for the protection of the integrity and legitimacy of the elections of 2022 and all future elections, from hereon.

We call upon Opposition leaders to lead the nation in gathering signatures for the People Mandamus. Only ordinary citizens have been laboring to gather signatures. And as of now we have only 20+ k signatures. But if the Opposition will assume leadership in this historic task of protecting our democracy, millions will sign the People Mandamus.

It is our most basic right and duty as citizens to protect the sanctity of our elections, which is the SOUL of our democracy. Once again we call the Opposition to lead the nation in making Comelec accountable to every Filipino voter!

....

15
Rosary and Novena in May 9, 2023 – Franklin Ysaac

A group photo with Sister Teresita Elevera, of Franciscan Sisters of Mary, who led the rosary and final novena for the truth in our election.

On behalf of the followers of this novena, we like to thank all the leaders who shared their time everyday from day 1 till 9th day.

It's mission accomplished according to one of our followers because our last day was held at the Manila Cathedral, home of the Immaculate Conception, the patron Saint of the Philippines.

We don't need a special miracle as everyday was a miracle as we gained many friends who believed in our mission.

In this photo are the followers of our daily rosary and novena with the Franciscan Sisters of Mary as our special guests.

We pray for you too Sisters and when we need to hold another novena we can count on you again.

May God grant our petition and our novena prayers

....

16

Leni should encourage her supporters to sign the mandamus petition – Franklin Ysaac – 5/12/23

The leading presidential bet, misled by her IT about election results, can now reverse her stand and claim the truth by endorsing the mandamus petition.

She owes her followers the strong bond that was generated during the many months of successful rallies.

This time, armed with the truth revealed to all, she can claim what she rightfully deserves as the people want her to lead.

The people don't deserve to be let down by their idol as they believed in her leadership.

Let this truth reach her ears as she won't be disappointed nor will she disappoint her million followers.

While our Truth campaign was non political, now that the truth is out, she can pick up the pieces that were shattered by the illegitimates.

You need to win back the faith and trust of those who lost their votes to the cheating by the regulators.

We turn over to this presidential bet the challenge that many of our followers are clamoring for her like Madame Cory who led us into the 1986 turnover after the same election fiasco by the disgraced dictator .

....

17
Nadaya si Leni – Hindi siya natalo. Iba yung daya sa talo. Posted in Tunay Na Pangulo is Leni Robreado Ph Group – May 12, 2023

NADAYA SI LENI

Kami ay nanawagan sa mga pulahan na itigil niyo na ang pagkakasabi kay Atty. Leni Robredo na siya ay "talo", sapagkat hindi lamang siya natalo, kundi nadaya. Ang panig naming mga taga-suporta ni Robredo ay naniniwala na siya ay dinadaya lamang, karamihan sa amin na sa bilangan ng halalan siya dinaya, dahil kaduda-duda ang 20 milyon sa loob ng isang oras na nagpalago sa boto ng inyong manok, hinihiling pa rin ng grupong TNTrio sa COMELEC na maglabas ng 'transmission log' upang malaman ang katotohanan; ngunit mas nakikita ng halos marami sa amin na ang pandaraya sa kanya ay hindi lamang sa bilangan ng halalan, kundi sa mga kasinungalingan, paninira, pekeng balita at 'red-tagging' laban sa kanya, na siyang umaakay sa nakararaming kababayan upang hindi siya ang pagkatiwalaan at iboto noong halalan.

Hinihimok din namin kayo na imbis na sumigaw kayo na "Talo si Leni" ay dapat gamitin niyo ng angkop ay ang "Dinaya si Leni" o "Nadaya si Leni", at kaming mga taga-suporta niya na sa halip na "talunan" ay gagamitin niyo sa amin ang "dinayaan" o "nadayaan". Tinatanggap man ni Robredo ang resulta ng halalan noong nakaraang taon, ngunit naniniwala pa rin kami na dinadaya lang talaga siya, kaya dapat niyong maintindihan ang sinasabi namin sa inyo.

Kung si Robredo sana ang nakaupo bilang Pangulo ng Pilipinas, matutupad nang matutupad ang kanyang mga magagandang pangako para sa sambayanang Pilipino, kagaya ng gobyernong tapat para umaangat ang pamumuhay nating lahat, ayuda o tulong para sa lahat, maayos na trabaho, paglutas ng mga suliranin o problema na kinakaharap ng bansa, palaguin ang ekonomiya at pag-unlad ng bansa, at sa paniniwala naming siya ang magkakapagbabalik sa tunay, disente at mabuting pamamahala, tuwid na daan, pagbabalik tiwala ng lahat sa gobyerno o pamahalaan, at daan para sa tunay na pagbabago at kinabukasan ng bansa at nating mga Pilipino.

#LeniRobredo #TunayNaPangulo #NadayaSiLeni #DinayaSiLeni #Pilipinas

....

18
No Politician or group is funding our legal team. Funds are solicited from the public to support our legal efforts – Franklin Ysaac – May 12, 2023

There are breaking news that we will be paid by a politician who is an enemy of the sitting and they are the ones giving us funds.

To tell the truth, we are not an organization or political party in the beginning. We just got together and shared our opinions about the last election . We don't have ambition and our actions are not politics but to make the election clean and transparent so that everyone will believe that there is no cheating.

It just happened that we are IT professionals and our question is the automated election that we think there is a miracle that happened that the 20M plus votes were counted in one hour.

Now, we can show in the graph they released that their graph is not factual and the Time stamps in the Election returns are different from the time stamps of transmission or reception reports they showed.

This questionable thing that they are showing is included in our discussion with our lawyer and there are additional cases.

Our followers who filed an impeachment and another complaint, we admire them. Please share their letters and complaints here. It means we are just not ready to file a case. They are our patriots Against election corruption .

Regarding the contribution we received and the Gofundme the money contribution is for the legal fund. That's why the Fight continues and we continue to pay our lawyers. We will not drop the case and we are ready to release our personal savings so we can Pay something to the lawyers .

That's really the case especially if we know that we are right and we won.

The legal fund is legit and the funds and payments to our lawyer have been published.

It's good that we got a good and experienced lawyer because it's hard for us to find at the beginning and many people we talked to don't want to be a lawyer because of conflict of interest.

God has provided us with good lawyers and we just pray that they continue to Handle the case until we win.

(Comments)

Rosalina Faustino
Laban lang po sir Franklin wag natin pansinin ang mga nanira na yan laki po talaga ng inggit sa TNTrio gusto kc ng taong nanira na yan na sya ang maging leader ng tntrio isa lang pong tao ang may sabi nyan wala pong nanira sa TNTrio dahil sila lang mismo ang gumagawa ng sarili nilang script para lang sirain ang trio

dahil ang taong yan ay hindi nya matanggao ang lahat dahil gusto nya talaga na sya ang makinabang ng lahat kaya hayaan niyo lang po ang nagsasabi ng paninira dahil sya mismo ang nanira laban lang hindi nila kayang sirain ang tntrio dahil ang tntrio ay para lang sa katotohanan walang political partisan at walang sino man na party list ang may hawak at ang TNTrio ay mga IT expert at mga professionals na mga tao at tanging laban lamang para sa katotohanan ang tunay na layunin alam na po ng taong yan kung sino sila..

....

19
Open Letter For Truth to Investigate Comelec Election Fraud in 2022 Elections – From North America Filam Groups – May 12, 2023

**OPEN LETTER
IMPLORING SUPPORT FOR THE PEOPLE'S FIGHT
FORTRUTH, TRANSPARENCY AND RIGHT TO
INFORMATION**

To:
Sen. Aquilino Pimentel
Sen. Risa Hontiveros
Sen. Juan M. Zubiri
Sen. Joel Villanueva
Rep. Jose Belmonte
Rep. Josephine Ramirez-Sato
Rep. Edcel Lagman
Rep. Rowena Guanzon
Ex-VP. Leonor G. Robredo

Ex-VP. Jejomar Binay
Ex-Sen. Francisco Pangitinan
Ex-Sen. Bam Aquino
Ex-Sen. Antonio Trillanes
Ex-Sen. Franklin Drilon
Ex-Sen. Richard Gordon
Ex-Sen. Manny Pacquiao
Ex-Sen. Ping Lacson
Ex-Sen. Mar Roxas
Ex-Rsp. Lorenzo Tanada III

Gov. Francis Escudero
Atty. Chel Diokno
Atty. Alex Lacson
Atty. Sonny Matula
Mr. Teddy Baguilat
Dr. Willie Ong
Mr. Lito Atienza
Mr. Mannv Lopez
Atty. Walden Bello
Mr. Carlos Serapio
Mr. Rizalito David
Mr. Isko Domagoso
Mr. Faisal Mangondato
Mr. Ernie Abella
Mr. Leody de Guzman
Mr. Norberto Gonzales
Mr. Jose Montemayor Jr.

Dear Sirs / Mdmes:

The Filipino people look up to you, as their representatives and putative leaders to champion and defend their constitutionally guaranteed right to information on matters bof public concern.

On November 3, 2022., **Messrs. Eliseo Rio Jr., Angusto Lagman, and FranklinYsaac (the 'TNTrio")** filed a Writ of Mandamus application before the

Supreme Court to compel the COMELEC to preserve relevant Vote Counting Machine ("VCM") transmission logs. These logs are required to confirm the truthfulness of

the voting results that COMELEC had reported during the first 2 hours of vote counting on May 9, 2022, which? after careful analysis, the TNTrio have determined to be statistically improbable and fraudulent.

The TNTrio had repeatedly requested COMELEC to make available the VCM transmission logs. However, COMELEC refused to grant their requests and gave them the run-around. This is a violation of the constitutionally guaranteed right of every Filipino citizen to information on matters of public concern and its own Resolution adopting the Policy of Freedom of Information.

Despite persistent public outcry winch include protests m front of COMELEC offices, online petitions and prayer rallies, COMELEC has failed to address the election rigging allegations in a prompt, transparent and forthright manner. It has been more than 6 months since the Mandamus petition was filed, yet COMELEC has not produced complete and verifiable evidence to corroborate the anomalous vote results it had reported.

The logs that COMELEC posted an its website on March 23, 2023 are not transmission logs but server reception logs. But there is something notable about the logs that demand an explanation. The logs actually substantiate the TNTrio's fraud allegations, as they show that vote results were being reported as received ahead of VCM transmissions! This is direct evidence of fraud that requires no less than a congressional investigation!

COMELEC's lack of transparency and continuing failure to address the TNTrio's allegations of vote result manipulation contradicts its mandate as the "vanguard of democracy" and "guardian of the people's voice". It is not fulfilling a duty it clearly owes the public: assuring voters of the integrity of the May 9 elections by releasing the documents or records required to substantiate the improbable election results that originated from its central computer servers.

The legal battle being waged by the TNTrio m the Supreme Court is not about determining who won the elections. Only the candidates directly affected can take that step. Rather, it is about upholding the Constitution and affirming the people's right to information on a matter of public concern - in this case, ascertaining the truth behind the highly questionable results that COMELEC reported on May 9. Success in this battle benefits all Filipinos, regardless of political affiliation. An affirmation of the people's right to information will do away with COMELEC's secretive and reticent conduct and will provide a safeguard against potential rigging of vote results in future elections. Recognizing this desirable outcome, more than 20,000 Filipinos have already signed an online petition supporting the TNTrio's Mandamus petition pending m the Supreme Court.

Through this letter, we implore you, in your roles as leaders and representatives, to act in the public interest and defend the people's right to information on matters of public concern, guaranteed by the Constitution (Article III Section 7).

Specifically, we ask you:

a. to speak out publicly, write letters or publish statements urging COMELEC to behave transparently perform its constitutional duty to the public and promptly comply with the TNTrio's demands for the release of genuine transmission logs and other information needed to verify the truthfulness of the questioned election results COMELEC reported during the first 2 hours of vote counting on May 9, 2022.

b. in light of the direct evidence of fraud that have been exposed by the TNTrio, initiate or urge a congressional or senate investigation into the palpable allegations of rigging of election results: and/or

c. encourage your supporters and followers to

demand complete transparency on the part of COMELEC by signing the People's Mandamus Petition.

By doing so, you will not only strengthen our democratic institutions and uphold the Constitution and rule of law but also restore the people's confidence and trust in government.

The fight for transparency is of transcendental importance to Filipinos. If you choose to remain silent and unsupportive of the people s right to information and their quest for truth and transparency, the people are likely to be disenchanted with your leadership and their disenchantment can only grow with every passing day that their demands are ignored by COMELEC. They will likely blame you for contributing to the demise of Philippine democracy with your silence, procrastination or indifference. It behooves you to consider what Martin Luther King Jr. said, "In the end, we will remember not the words of our enemies, but the silence of our friends."

Signed by:

GLOBAL PINOY DIASPORA CANADA (Vancouver, British Columbia, Can.)
PAMANA CULTURAL ASSOCIATION (Toronto, Ontario, Canada)
DAMAYAN MIGRANT WORKERS (New York City, New York, USA)
1521 SOLIDARITY FOR TRUTH AND JUSTICE (Manila, PhiHppmes)

OPEN LETTER IMPLORING SUPPORT FOR THE PEOPLE'S FIGHT FOR TRUTH, TRANSPARENCY AND RIGHT TO INFORMATION

TO:

Sen. Aquilino Pimentel	Gov. Francis Escudero
Sen. Risa Hontiveros	Atty. Chel Diokno
Sen. Juan M. Zubiri	Atty. Alex Lacson
Sen. Joel Villanueva	Atty. Sonny Matula
Rep. Jose Belmonte	Mr. Teddy Baguilat
Rep. Josephine Ramirez-Sato	Dr. Willie Ong
Rep. Edcel Lagman	Mr. Lito Atienza
Rep. Rowena Guanzon	Mr. Manny Lopez
Ex-V.P. Leonor G. Robredo	Atty. Walden Bello
Ex-V.P. Jejomar Binay	Mr. Carlos Serapio
Ex-Sen. Francisco Pangilinan	Mr. Rizalito David
Ex-Sen. Bam Aquino	Mr. Isko Domagoso
Ex-Sen. Antonio Trillanes	Mr. Faisal Mangondato
Ex-Sen. Franklin Drilon	Mr. Ernie Abella
Ex-Sen. Richard Gordon	Mr. Leody de Guzman
Ex-Sen. Manny Pacquiao	Mr. Norberto Gonzales
Ex-Sen. Ping Lacson	Mr. Jose Montemayor, Jr.
Ex-Sen. Mar Roxas	
Ex-Rep. Lorenzo Tanada III	

Dear Sirs / Mdmes:

The Filipino people look up to you, as their representatives and putative leaders, to champion and defend their constitutionally guaranteed right to information on matters of public concern.

On November 3, 2022, Messrs. Eliseo Rio Jr., Augusto Lagman, and Franklin Ysaac (the "TNTrio") filed a Writ of Mandamus application before the Supreme Court, to compel the COMELEC to preserve relevant Vote Counting Machine ("VCM") transmission logs. These logs are required to confirm the truthfulness of the voting results that COMELEC had reported during the first 2 hours of vote counting on May 9, 2022, which, after careful analysis, the TNTrio have determined to be statistically improbable and fraudulent.

The TNTrio had repeatedly requested COMELEC to make available the VCM transmission logs. However, COMELEC refused to grant their requests and gave them the run-around. This is a violation of the constitutionally guaranteed right

1

of every Filipino citizen to information on matters of public concern and its own Resolution adopting the Policy of Freedom of Information.

Despite persistent public outcry, which include protests in front of COMELEC offices, online petitions and prayer rallies, COMELEC has failed to address the election rigging allegations in a prompt, transparent and forthright manner. It has been more than 6 months since the Mandamus petition was filed, yet COMELEC has not produced complete and verifiable evidence to corroborate the anomalous vote results it had reported.

The logs that COMELEC posted on its website on March 23, 2023 are not transmission logs but server reception logs. But there is something notable about the logs that demand an explanation. The logs actually substantiate the TNTrio's fraud allegations, as they show that vote results were being reported as received ahead of VCM transmissions! This is direct evidence of fraud that requires no less than a congressional investigation.'

COMELEC's lack of transparency and continuing failure to address the TNTrio's allegations of vote result manipulation contradicts its mandate as the "vanguard of democracy" and "guardian of the people's votes". It is not fulfilling a duty it clearly owes the public: assuring voters of the integrity of the May 9 elections by releasing the documents or records required to substantiate the improbable election results that originated from its central computer servers.

The legal battle being waged by the TNTrio in the Supreme Court is not about determining who won the elections. Only the candidates directly affected can take that step. Rather, it is about **upholding the Constitution and affirming the people's right to information on a matter of public concern** – in this case, ascertaining the truth behind the highly questionable results that COMELEC reported on May 9. Success in this battle benefits all Filipinos, regardless of political affiliation. An affirmation of the people's right to information will do away with COMELEC's secretive and reticent conduct and will provide a safeguard against potential rigging of vote results in future elections. Recognizing this desirable outcome, more than 50,000 Filipinos have already signed an online petition supporting the TNTrio's Mandamus petition pending in the Supreme Court.

Through this letter, we implore you, in your roles as leaders and representatives, to act in the public interest and defend the people's right to information on matters of public concern, guaranteed by the Constitution (Article III, Section 7).

2

Specifically, we ask you:

a. to speak out publicly, write letters or publish statements urging COMELEC to behave transparently, perform its constitutional duty to the public and promptly comply with the TNTrio's demands for the release of genuine transmission logs and other information needed to verify the truthfulness of the questioned election results COMELEC reported during the first 2 hours of vote counting on May 9;

b. in light of the direct evidence of fraud that have been exposed by the TNTrio, initiate or urge a congressional or senate investigation into the palpable allegations of rigging of election results and/or

c. encourage your supporters and followers to demand complete transparency on the part of COMELEC by signing the People's Mandamus Petition.

By doing so, you will not only strengthen our democratic institutions and uphold the Constitution and rule of law but also restore the people's confidence and trust in government.

The fight for transparency is of transcendental importance to Filipinos. If you choose to remain silent and unsupportive of the people's right to information and their quest for truth and transparency, the people are likely to be disenchanted with your leadership, and their disenchantment can only grow with every passing day that their demands are ignored by COMELEC. They will likely blame you for contributing to the demise of Philippine democracy with your silence, procrastination or indifference. It behooves you to consider what Martin Luther King Jr. said, "In the end, we will remember not the words of our enemies, but the silence of our friends."

Signed by:

GLOBAL PINOY DIASPORA CANADA (Vancouver, British Columbia, Canada)
PAMANA CULTURAL ASSOCIATION (Toronto, Ontario, Canada)
DAMAYAN MIGRANT WORKERS (New York City, New York, USA)
1521 SOLIDARITY FOR TRUTH AND JUSTICE (Manila, Philippines)

20
Bigo pero magdasal tayo - Posted at facebook by Beth Flora – May 10, 2023

Kagaya ng marami, umasa rin ako na gaganda at magiging matino ang gobyerno natin pagkatapos ng eleksiyon noong May 9, 2022.

Ang masaklap, nabigo at di ko matanggap ang resulta ng bilangan,nagkaroon ako ng depression-para bang nawalan ng pag-asa ang bayan ko at nawala rin ang pagmamahal at respeto, lalo na ang mga taga COMOLEC in the sanctity of the ballot

It took months bago ako nagising that the election was really rigged!!!

But THANK GOD, prayer indeed works!

He showed me TNTrio's posts, nitong 2023 na, and started following/interacting via fb.

I believe TNTrio+1 are God's chosen to lead us into the truth and transparency of last year's elections.

We may not understand why God has allowed that election fraud happened, but let us trust in Him-in His goodness and wisdom

He is an all-powerful God, He sees the suffering and sacrifices of His people, and He will not let us in vain

He will bring forth justice to the Filipino people!

All glory and honor belongs to Him, my Lord and my God

Let us rejoice in the hope that God shall bring forth redemption for the Filipinos, in His time, in His loving grace

Lord, please have mercy on Your people

Let us humble ourselves, repent, and turn away from wicked ways

Lord, thank You for TNTrio+1;

Thank you for all Your blessings, please supply TNTrio the strength, courage, wisdom and good health to lead us in this endeavor❣

We need Your divine providence and protection, oh Lord, let us persevere in Your truth, way, and light❣

In Jesus' name we pray, AMEN❣❣❣

Filipinos deserve the truth, justice, and good governance❣

God bless the Philippines❣

Mabuhay ang Pilipino❣

🙏🙏🙏❀❀

....

21
Legal battle – Franklin Ysaac – May 10, 2023

May 10, 2022, It's the morning after the traumatic wipeout of Filipino hopes for a better life under a credible presidency.

One year later, after millions have given up hopes of reversing the incredulous election results, we never gave up hope.

While we were making small rounds, holding interviews, making prescon, not too many dared to offer help, not even the mainstream press attempted to share our views about irregularities.

We did our share of exposing the lies and pinning the burden on regulators who didn't even lift fingers in answering our queries about transmission logs.

To the credit of some of our followers and to the fiasco committed after the regulators opened up with their disclosure of the questionable numbers did we file the mandamus petition.

We made it clear to SC that our petition was not a political protest but an expression of our civic rights as voters to know the truth and to force the regulators to tell us the truth about the conduct of the election which was not fair, honest and transparent. It was a simple request to preserve the election data .

One by one, after our mandamus was listened to by SC, the regulators through their lawyer responded with a delaying tactic and even exposing further more untruths as they published two conflicting transmission logs and mismatched ER and Tranmission logs time stamps .

Thereafter, we filed supplemental petition to compel the regulators answer this big discrepancy.

It's very obvious that since they cannot cover up their lies, they resorted to delaying tactics and for the JCOCAE, they conveniently made another excuse that they have not met even if they were mandated by law to meet after 6 months .

Now, the telcos and smartmatic are also failing as they have not even answered the SC order . Defiant, they are in effect waiving their rights as we will make the necessary manifestation and motion with SC with regard to their non reply.

This is now a battle for legal supremacy as better legal minds, with truth as weapon, will win this case .

Let's pray that our lawyers will be guided by the Holy Spirit as they appear before SC defending our case, defending the truth and defending our constitutional right to know the truth .

Holy Spirit, please keep us strong and faithful to thee.

Amen .

....

22
Analysis by US-based IT Filipino Person – Eliseo Rio Jr. – May 9, 2023

An IT Filipino Patriot based in the United States was able to acutely analyzed the Reception Logs uploaded by COMELEC in its website last March 23, 2023. He discovered a highly statistically improbable if NOT IMPOSSIBLE constant ratio of voters who actually voted to the registered voters in precincts nationwide grouped by provinces. There is absolutely no relationship or any connection whatsoever in the actual number who actually voted in a precinct when compared with another precinct. More so would there be any correlation on the number of actual voters that voted in the first hour when compared to those who voted in the second hour.

But the IMPOSSIBLE happened in the 2022 Election in the Philippines! Nationwide, the ratio of actual voters to registered voters in clustered precincts remained the same in the second hour at 84%, exactly the same 84% as in the first hour. And in that first two hours "tapos na Ang boksing" for the Presidency and VP. The only way this can happen is when the ELECTION IS RIGGED!

Here is a list of Provinces whose ratio of actual voters to registered voters did not changed at ALL from the first hour to the second hour:-
1. Agusan Del Norte - 85%, 85%
2. Agusan Del Sur - 83%, 83%
3. Aklan - 86%, 86%
4. Antique - 87%, 87%
5. Apayao - 87%, 87%
6. Bataan - 88%, 88%

7. Batanes - 85%, 85%
8. Batangas- 87%, 87%
9. Bohol - 88%, 88%
10. Bukidnon - 88%, 88%
11. Bulacan - 88%, 88%
12. Cagayan - 85%, 85%
13. Cam Norte - 87%, 87%
14. Cam Sur - 86%, 86%
15. Camiguin - 86%,86%
16. Capiz - 86%, 86%
17. Catanduanes - 87%, 87%
18. Cebu - 86%, 86%
19. Davao Norte - 83%, 83%
20. Davao Oriental - 86%, 86%
21. Eastern Samar - 84%, 84%
22. Guimaras - 87%, 87%
23. Leyte - 87%, 87%
24. Marinduque - 87%, 87%
25. Masbate - 83%, 83%
26. Misamis Or - 87%, 87%
27. NCR-3rd Dist - 82%, 82%
28. NCR-4th Dist - 82%, 82%
29. Negros Occ - 85%, 85%
30. Negros Or - 85%, 85%
31. Nueva Vizcaya - 85%, 85%
32. Occ Mindoro - 84%, 84%
33. Or Mindoro - 82%, 82%
34. Pampanga -87%, 87%
35. Pangasinan - 87%, 87%
36. Romblon - 85%, 85%
37. Samar - 85%, 85%
38. Siquijor - 88%, 88%
39. Sorsogon - 87%, 87%
40. Sultan Kudarat - 80%, 80%
41. Surigao Del Norte - 86%, 86%
42. Surigao Del Sur - 88%, 88%
43. Tarlac - 88%, 88%
44. Zamboanga Del Sur -81%, 81%

RECEPTION LOGS ACTUAL VOTES BY PROVINCE BY HOUR

| PROVINCE | 1ST HOUR | | | | 2ND HOUR | | | |
| | 09-May-2022 19:08:50 to 09-May-2022 20:02:00 | | | | 09-May-2022 20:02:01 to 09-May-2022 21:00:00 | | | |
	TOTAL VCMs	ACTUAL VOTES	CLUSTER TOTAL	%	TOTAL VCMs	ACTUAL VOTES	CLUSTER TOTAL	%
ABRA	164	66,601	76,675	87%	94	42,744	48,744	88%
AGUSAN DEL NORTE	214	118,212	139,084	85%	191	105,416	123,909	85%
AGUSAN DEL SUR	140	70,600	85,211	83%	126	67,735	81,672	83%
AKLAN	145	72,310	84,152	86%	233	122,091	142,585	86%
ALBAY	538	273,965	313,081	88%	374	194,342	223,052	87%
AMERICAS	0	0	0	0%	1	953	2,000	48%
ANTIQUE	161	69,546	80,175	87%	180	82,529	94,841	87%
APAYAO	40	17,429	20,126	87%	35	14,425	16,646	87%
ASIA PACIFIC	11	7,520	11,629	65%	5	3,863	6,000	64%
AURORA	101	48,060	56,996	84%	66	30,655	36,223	85%
BASILAN	20	8,553	12,686	67%	40	17,826	24,405	73%
BATAAN	383	216,944	246,975	88%	325	189,776	215,233	88%
BATANES	12	4,846	5,701	85%	14	4,919	5,778	85%
BATANGAS	1,919	1,061,401	1,217,115	87%	593	332,419	379,929	87%
BENGUET	403	191,170	227,035	84%	217	97,114	112,962	86%
BILIRAN	71	34,042	40,702	84%	54	26,421	31,153	85%
BOHOL	492	225,080	255,654	88%	418	207,975	236,052	88%
BUKIDNON	320	175,323	202,538	87%	385	218,322	252,321	87%
BULACAN	816	488,660	555,990	88%	801	493,005	561,666	88%
CAGAYAN	573	270,042	316,787	85%	393	188,761	221,128	85%
CAMARINES NORTE	223	112,352	129,245	87%	188	100,022	114,333	87%
CAMARINES SUR	708	350,453	408,637	86%	634	328,562	382,383	86%
CAMIGUIN	27	12,971	14,997	86%	38	17,700	20,616	86%
CAPIZ	268	136,319	158,154	86%	215	112,441	129,995	86%
CATANDUANES	147	59,495	68,165	87%	113	48,751	55,870	87%
CAVITE	2,466	1,350,852	1,665,833	81%	662	377,884	461,528	82%
CEBU	1,492	896,122	1,043,806	86%	1,263	770,765	893,450	86%
COTOBATO	320	163,338	195,020	84%	367	187,829	225,323	83%
DAVAO DEL ORO	129	70,491	80,639	87%	150	85,408	97,585	88%
DAVAO DEL NORTE	188	104,428	125,499	83%	220	127,261	152,479	83%
DAVAO DEL SUR	833	442,553	590,093	75%	462	250,270	325,402	77%
DAVAO OCCIDENTAL	40	18,739	24,653	76%	45	21,824	28,114	78%
DAVAO ORIENTAL	119	65,403	75,812	86%	102	57,249	66,298	86%
DINAGAT ISLANDS	30	11,976	14,719	81%	28	12,043	14,581	83%
EASTERN SAMAR	278	100,677	119,648	84%	175	72,052	85,687	84%
EUROPE	0	0	0	0%	0	0	0	0%
GUIMARAS	45	23,428	26,958	87%	42	21,147	24,267	87%
IFUGAO	109	45,795	55,044	83%	53	22,676	26,849	84%
ILOCOS NORTE	346	157,376	180,412	87%	317	150,480	170,845	88%
ILOCOS SUR	540	226,159	254,449	89%	247	106,961	118,943	90%
ILOILO	1,088	512,084	610,724	84%	798	375,575	443,358	85%
ISABELA	905	440,409	530,031	83%	467	229,654	274,853	84%
KALINGA	79	36,485	41,316	88%	84	40,906	46,793	87%
LA UNION	552	267,122	305,988	87%	243	124,059	140,916	88%
LAGUNA	1,472	799,669	993,923	80%	913	506,440	625,559	81%
LANAO DEL NORTE	291	138,938	170,510	81%	246	121,482	146,454	83%
LANAO DEL SUR	63	25,368	31,418	81%	92	36,778	44,289	83%
LEYTE	860	385,434	443,807	87%	691	328,728	376,964	87%
MAGUINDANAO	162	68,422	101,089	68%	194	86,916	121,472	72%
MARINDUQUE	116	52,761	60,943	87%	83	39,096	44,887	87%
MASBATE	185	92,330	111,687	83%	192	93,836	112,730	83%
MIDDLE EAST AND AFRICAS	0	0	0	0%	4	2,248	4,000	56%
MISAMIS OCCIDENTAL	252	114,982	136,382	84%	182	86,329	101,790	85%
MISAMIS ORIENTAL	439	240,739	278,002	87%	412	234,138	269,753	87%
MOUNTAIN PROVINCE	83	34,272	42,073	81%	60	22,697	27,334	83%
NCR-4TH DISTRICT	1,859	1,055,984	1,288,776	82%	712	422,118	514,779	82%
NCR-MANILA	1,364	634,333	814,937	78%	275	139,735	175,131	80%
NCR-2ND DISTRICT	2,213	1,299,105	1,583,261	82%	657	400,386	484,130	83%
NCR-3RD DISTRICT	1,709	985,034	1,201,670	82%	286	171,133	208,581	82%
NEGROS OCCIDENTAL	972	545,965	644,995	85%	871	495,711	585,470	85%
NEGROS ORIENTAL	300	155,641	182,706	85%	322	174,076	204,039	85%
NORTHERN SAMAR	198	86,950	107,929	81%	114	52,759	64,689	82%
NUEVA ECIJA	1,017	547,585	654,467	84%	739	407,425	482,089	85%
NUEVA VIZCAYA	163	81,357	95,377	85%	139	70,958	83,487	85%
OCCIDENTAL MINDORO	167	86,573	102,958	84%	125	66,031	78,732	84%
ORIENTAL MINDORO	358	178,127	216,801	82%	290	141,354	171,846	82%
PALAWAN	406	198,966	238,537	83%	264	136,279	162,623	84%
PAMPANGA	536	305,773	349,488	87%	688	399,095	458,746	87%
PANGASINAN	1,423	773,889	889,050	87%	984	536,620	616,013	87%
QUEZON	556	278,032	325,948	85%	528	279,002	325,266	86%
QUIRINO	68	33,007	38,464	86%	66	33,402	39,234	85%
RIZAL	854	480,614	589,234	82%	898	508,782	633,556	80%
ROMBLON	137	65,084	76,323	85%	64	32,555	38,297	85%
SAMAR	254	106,071	125,024	85%	217	93,918	110,892	85%
SARANGANI	123	61,002	79,721	77%	115	56,409	73,834	76%
SIQUIJOR	34	14,032	15,988	88%	38	16,230	18,494	88%
SORSOGON	300	145,112	166,732	87%	207	109,886	126,042	87%
SOUTH COTABATO	459	246,712	310,858	79%	396	218,486	270,966	81%
SOUTHERN LEYTE	242	97,096	112,092	87%	124	53,797	62,398	86%
SULTAN KUDARAT	164	81,594	101,499	80%	217	110,143	137,831	80%
SULU	76	35,142	42,581	83%	84	41,433	47,511	87%
SURIGAO DEL NORTE	179	85,313	99,434	86%	140	72,396	83,960	86%
SURIGAO DEL SUR	124	61,159	69,761	88%	99	51,704	58,848	88%
TARLAC	544	296,789	338,797	88%	503	287,014	327,803	88%
TAWI-TAWI	41	20,113	25,911	78%	58	27,585	34,921	79%
ZAMBALES	359	193,911	230,172	84%	249	141,929	166,341	85%
ZAMBOANGA DEL NORTE	294	137,605	170,162	81%	196	94,993	115,548	82%
ZAMBOANGA DEL SUR	476	243,397	300,123	81%	479	248,154	306,760	81%
ZAMBOANGA SIBUGAY	167	81,552	102,098	80%	113	53,391	66,006	81%
TOTAL	39,512	20,676,855	24,729,842	84%	25,784	13,786,387	16,326,862	84%

....

23
Offer to run the election system in the future – Franklin Ysaac – May 9, 2023

In my two minute discourse before the rallyist crowd yesterday before the Comelec, I dared the Comelec to allow TNTrio to set up and run a clean, transparent automated election system. I even offered our services for free unlike the P50B they are proposing again for replacement of VCM!

As IT with experience in handling a simple automated election system, TNTrio has the capacity and capability to make a transparent and credible election system. We will make room for recommendations from other IT experts to join us in this challenge.

Government will save billions from this generous offer.

That's our contribution for a clean and honest election. No more frauds!

NASUSUKOL NA ANG COMELEC
KUMIKILOS NA ANG SAMBAYANAN
31M
WRIT OF #SupportTNTrio
MANDAMUS
PETITION
#Telcos
#Comelec
#Smartmatic
#HocusPocus
MR. ELISEO RIO, JR.
FORMER DICT ACTING SECRETARY
MR. FRANKLIN YSAAC
FORMER PHEX PRESIDENT
MR. GUS LAGMAN
FORMER COMELEC AND NAMFREL CHAIRMAN
COMELEC RELEASE THE TRUE TRANSMISSION LOGS NOW!
The inconsistencies in the statements of COMELEC significantly erode the credibility of the 2022 Election.
Inconsistency #1
20M+ votes counted PEAKED at 1st hour while VCM transmissions PEAKED at 2nd hour.
Inconsistency #2
Making transmission logs public will violate the sanctity of the ballot yet these were made public on March 23.
Inconsistency #3
COMELEC said it will make transmission logs public but what it published are reception logs.
Inconsistency #4
COMELEC said it will investigate Namfrel's discovery of change in the VCM source code. It never did.
Inconsistency #5
COMELEC said the results shown in the Transparency Server came from PPCRV. PPCRV opposed this.
Inconsistency #6
COMELEC configured SD cards illegally without any witnesses, using COVID protocols as flimsy excuse.
Inconsistency #7
COMELEC claim accuracy observed by election watchdogs, but they can't independently verify.
Bukod sa COMMISSIONER, mga DOKTOR din pala sila.
EM
ctto

COMELEC, tunay na Transmission Logs ilabas!
SMARTMAGIC
COMMISSION ON ELECTIONS
REPUBLIC OF THE PHILIPPINES
#Telcos
#Comelec
#Smartmatic
#HocusPocus
TULOY-TULOY NA
NAGBIGAY NG
LIWANAG SA DILIM
#SupportTNTrio

24
Col. Odono Official Request to Comelec – Franklin Ysaac – May 10, 2023

Breaking news!

After the 9th day of our novena at the Manila Cathedral and after the mass and rally before the Comelec yesterday, one of our followers, Col Odono filed this request with Comelec.

The specifics are mentioned and the request includes inhibition of the commissioners involved in the May 2022 anomalous election.

This request seeks impartiality as only the new commissioners can decide.

The follow up includes mention of court of appeals action if the mentioned and inhibited commissioners question this request.

The battleground, as I said, has shifted to the legal court and we expect more action in the forthcoming days.

As they say, they can try to hide the truth using press releases but they cannot hide from court subpoenas and they will be kept busy answering a barrage of new charges in the SC, ombudsman, CA and regular courts.

They will have their day in court not in their air conditioned rooms and offices.

28 April 2023

Chairman George Erwin Mojica Garcia
Commissioner Socorro Balinghasay Inting
Commissioner Marlon Sabucido Casquejo
Commissioner Aimee Ferolino Ampoloquio
Commissioner Rey Echavarria Bulay
Commissioner Nelson Java Celis
Commissioner Ernesto Vera Perez Maceda
COMMISSION ON ELECTIONS (COMELEC)
<clerkofthecommission@comelec.gov.ph>
Palacio del Gobernador Building ‹ Intramuros ‹ Manila

Your Honors:

This is a follow-up to my earlier constitutional-right-to-know and freedom of information (FOI) request for **Transmission** Data Logs = not **Reception** Data Logs such as the one given to me last 23 March 2023. No less than the COMELEC website expressly labels it as the "List of VCM **Received** Transmission Logs". Hence the time stamps there report the time of **receipt** by the Central Server instead of the more important time of **transmission** by the vote counting machines or VCM nationwide. The said 23 March 2023 reception data logs contain numerous embarrassments such as the significant number of VCM transmission reports with time stamps reporting transmission times that came **after** (instead of before) their respective reception time by the Central Server and/or Transparency Server.

I therefore respectfully request for a simple win-win compromise solution by just simply allowing the telecommunication companies (DITO Tele-community & Globe Telecom & Smart Communications) to disclose their copies of the very same data that is the subject matter of this lawful request for the People.

I likewise respectfully request for *delicadeza* in the resolution of this request. Undeniably, the COMELEC Chairman and the first four Commissioners cannot resolve this request with cold impartial neutrality. The said Chairman and first four Commissioners must therefore voluntarily inhibit from the En Banc deliberation for the approval or disapproval of this request. *Delicadeza* voluntary inhibitions by five-out-of-seven in the En Banc may result to apparent lack of quorum but that is not a problem because the Administrative Code provides for a solution wherein the COURT OF APPEALS (CA) Presiding Justice shall designate a CA Justice or CA Justices who shall join Commissioner Nelson Java Celis and Commissioner Ernesto Vera Perez Maceda in constituting a special quorum that shall resolve the particularly specific issue pertaining to transmission versus reception data logs. Please refer to the Administrative Code specifically in (Book V) (Title I = Constitutional Commissions) (Sub-Title C = COMELEC) (Chapter 2 = En Banc) (Section 6).

Cordially

Colonel **Leonardo** Olivera **Odoño** (retired)
Philippine Military Academy Class of 1964
<colloo64@yahoo.com>

Copy sent to the COURT OF APPEALS Presiding Justice
<coc.ca@judiciary.gov.ph>

. . . .

25
As they say, " Complacency is the enemy of success"! – Franklin Ysaac – May 14, 2023

We have been complacent for more than 20 years and we let that tenant ruin and run our country to the ground.

Waking up one day after the exiled true leader was gunned down, complacency was gone. Then the tenant was finally ousted in a peaceful change in 1986.

Then, after memories of 1986 have slipped away, return to complacency has settled again in the populace who returned the power back to the namesake.

Whereas, in 1986, we were the model of peaceful political change by the world , now, 37 years later, we are the model of political amnesia.

We have become again the pariah, the epitome of the same people who were complacent for 20 long years.

What will change this complacency is beyond this discourse as the true leader has not returned after failing to win a legit election.

What will it take to prod true leaders to take the handle or the staff and assemble the same people who entrusted their faith with said leaders and to declare to the whole world we are not a pariah anymore ?

We are what we should be 37 years ago who will not allow continuance of illegitimate leaders.

The ball is in the true leader's hands.

Please handle the truth with care and wisdom so we will embrace the truth we once lost and redeemed in 1986.

The next election is 5 years away and if we let complacency be our future, then let's suffer more the next 5 years of illegitimacy,

Complacency will become the synonym of illegitimacy!!!

....

26
Tansmission Logs supported by Telco Call Data Records (CDEs) – Eliseo Rio Jr. – May 14, 2023

In a clean and honest election, any data shown to the public by COMELEC must be consistently within reasonably accurate bounds.

Comparing the data updates from the COMELEC Transparency Server shown to the public from 7pm of May 9, 2022 to the afternoon of of March 13, 2022, to the data of Received VCM transmissions shown in the Reception Logs uploaded by COMELEC in their website on March 23, 2023, one will immediately notice that the Transparency Server was receiving data from VCM transmissions in the 2023 upload FASTER than what was being shown to the public in May, 2022. The difference went as high as more than 2M actual votes. Such discrepancies should not happen in a highly technical automated system that we paid billions of pesos to insure accuracy in our election. Such discrepancies can only happen when the system was RIGGED.

This shows how important it is for COMELEC to show ACTUAL TRANSMISSION LOGS corroborated by Telcos' Call Data Records (CDRs), for the data shown the public on May 2022, DO NOT MATCH the data uploaded to the COMELEC website on March 2023, supposedly of the same received VCM transmissions. COMELEC continued refusal to show the Transmission Logs is proof enough that they are hiding something.

	A	B	C	D
1	Date/Time	Total (Transparency Server, May 9-13)	Total (Transparency Server, March 23,2023)	Difference between the two data
2	May 9/7:00pm	0	0	0
3	May 9/7:17pm	1,525,637	1,350,742	174,895
4	May 9/8:02pm	20,061,691	20,668,384	606,693
5	May9/8:17pm	25,459,825	26,356,174	896,349
6	May9/8:32pm	29,096,429	30,236,160	1,139,731
7	May9/8:47pm	31,469,898	32,729,938	1,260,040
8	May9/9:02pm	33,310,321	34,682,958	1,372,637
9	May9/9:17pm	34,239,232	36,283,877	2,044,645
10	May9/9:32pm	36,080,534	37,621,250	1,540,716
11	May9/9:47pm	37,239,232	38,856,168	1,616,936
12	May9/10:02pm	38,280,810	39,964,942	1,684,132
13	May9/10:17pm	39,204,447	40,965,624	1,761,177
14	May9/10:32pm	40,108,140	41,926,338	1,818,198
15	May9/10:47pm	40,966,010	42,847,761	1,881,751
16	May9/11:02pm	41,802,484	43,744,401	1,941,917
17	May9/11:17pm	42,571,345	44,583,993	2,012,648
18	May10/5:32am	50,778,545	53,487,139	2,708,594
19	May13/3:18pm	52,338,277	NO RECORD	NO RECORD
20				

....

27
Comelec Results Full of Discrepansies – Eliseo Rio Jr – May 16, 2023

The Reception Logs uploaded in COMELEC's website last March 23, 2023, shown to the public are full of discrepancies. The 7:08 pm start of receptions is IMPOSSIBLE because it took 12 minutes just to print 8 copies of the Election Returns (ERs) and another 7 minutes to finish the other administrative tasks required to be completed BEFORE any VCM transmissions can begin. There were several ERs that were received in the Transparency Server even before these were transmitted by the precinct VCMs. There were statistically IMPOSSIBLE data where the ratio of actual voters to registered voters are the same in several provinces and do not change in two successive hours. The Transmission Logs shown on October 18, 2022 do NOT match the Reception Logs shown on March 23, 2023. There are 113 Oversea precincts that have exactly 1,000 registered voters with all 1,000 actually voting or all having 100% voter's turnout.

And in spite of all these highly questionable and unbelievable data, COMELEC says that the 2022 Election was the best ever in our history. The election watchdogs never saw any irregularities at all. Yet, COMELEC is scrambling to buy more expensive voting machines with more rigid specifications to replace the most efficient Automated Election System ever. WHY spend more money on a system that is already perfect? Exactly whom are they fooling?

CLUSTERED	ACTUAL	RECEPTION DATETIME	REGION	PROVINCE	MUNICIPALITY	BARANGAY	PRECINCT_ID	CLUSTERTOTAL	POLLINGCENTER
90010106	1,000	09-May-2022 20:48:22	OAV	ASIA PACIFIC	PEOPLES REPUBLIC OF CHINA	MACAU PCG	90010106	1000	MACAU PCG, PEOPLES REPUBLIC OF CHINA
90030021	1,000	09-May-2022 23:08:14	OAV	ASIA PACIFIC	PEOPLES REPUBLIC OF CHINA	HONGKONG PCG	90030021	1000	HONGKONG PCG, PEOPLES REPUBLIC OF CHINA
90030081	1,000	09-May-2022 21:30:02	OAV	ASIA PACIFIC	PEOPLES REPUBLIC OF CHINA	HONGKONG PCG	90030081	1000	HONGKONG PCG, PEOPLES REPUBLIC OF CHINA
90030091	1,000	09-May-2022 21:22:41	OAV	ASIA PACIFIC	PEOPLES REPUBLIC OF CHINA	HONGKONG PCG	90030091	1000	HONGKONG PCG, PEOPLES REPUBLIC OF CHINA
90010841	1,000	09-May-2022 21:38:21	OAV	ASIA PACIFIC	PEOPLES REPUBLIC OF CHINA	HONGKONG PCG	90030041	1000	HONGKONG PCG, PEOPLES REPUBLIC OF CHINA
90030051	1,000	09-May-2022 21:41:21	OAV	ASIA PACIFIC	PEOPLES REPUBLIC OF CHINA	HONGKONG PCG	90030051	1000	HONGKONG PCG, PEOPLES REPUBLIC OF CHINA
90010107	1,000	09-May-2022 21:42:33	OAV	ASIA PACIFIC	PEOPLES REPUBLIC OF CHINA	MACAU PCG	90010107	1000	MACAU PCG, PEOPLES REPUBLIC OF CHINA
90030061	1,000	09-May-2022 21:44:44	OAV	ASIA PACIFIC	PEOPLES REPUBLIC OF CHINA	HONGKONG PCG	90030061	1000	HONGKONG PCG, PEOPLES REPUBLIC OF CHINA
90010012	1,000	09-May-2022 21:47:51	OAV	ASIA PACIFIC	PEOPLES REPUBLIC OF CHINA	HONGKONG PCG	90030012	1000	HONGKONG PCG, PEOPLES REPUBLIC OF CHINA
90110001	1,000	09-May-2022 21:52:12	OAV	ASIA PACIFIC	MALAYSIA	KUALA LUMPUR PE	90110001	1000	KUALA LUMPUR PE, MALAYSIA
90030022	1,000	09-May-2022 22:07:16	OAV	ASIA PACIFIC	PEOPLES REPUBLIC OF CHINA	HONGKONG PCG	90030022	1000	HONGKONG PCG, PEOPLES REPUBLIC OF CHINA
92010011	1,000	09-May-2022 22:15:04	OAV	MIDDLE EAST AND AFRICAS	UNITED ARAB EMIRATES	ABU DHABI PE	92010011	1000	ABU DHABI PE, UNITED ARAB EMIRATES
90160068	1,000	09-May-2022 22:16:19	OAV	ASIA PACIFIC	REPUBLIC OF SINGAPORE	SINGAPORE PE	90160068	1000	SINGAPORE PE, REPUBLIC OF SINGAPORE
92010005	2,000	09-May-2022 22:23:51	OAV	MIDDLE EAST AND AFRICAS	UNITED ARAB EMIRATES	ABU DHABI PE	92010005	1000	ABU DHABI PE, UNITED ARAB EMIRATES
90030062	1,000	09-May-2022 22:28:00	OAV	ASIA PACIFIC	PEOPLES REPUBLIC OF CHINA	HONGKONG PCG	90030062	1000	HONGKONG PCG, PEOPLES REPUBLIC OF CHINA
90030002	1,000	09-May-2022 22:31:22	OAV	ASIA PACIFIC	PEOPLES REPUBLIC OF CHINA	HONGKONG PCG	90030002	1000	HONGKONG PCG, PEOPLES REPUBLIC OF CHINA
92010002	1,000	09-May-2022 22:36:48	OAV	MIDDLE EAST AND AFRICAS	UNITED ARAB EMIRATES	ABU DHABI PE	92010002	1000	ABU DHABI PE, UNITED ARAB EMIRATES
90030072	1,000	09-May-2022 22:45:12	OAV	ASIA PACIFIC	PEOPLES REPUBLIC OF CHINA	HONGKONG PCG	90030072	1000	HONGKONG PCG, PEOPLES REPUBLIC OF CHINA
90110002	1,000	09-May-2022 22:47:16	OAV	ASIA PACIFIC	MALAYSIA	KUALA LUMPUR PE	90110002	1000	KUALA LUMPUR PE, MALAYSIA
90030013	1,000	09-May-2022 22:57:50	OAV	ASIA PACIFIC	PEOPLES REPUBLIC OF CHINA	HONGKONG PCG	90030013	1000	HONGKONG PCG, PEOPLES REPUBLIC OF CHINA
90160036	1,000	09-May-2022 23:02:31	OAV	ASIA PACIFIC	REPUBLIC OF SINGAPORE	SINGAPORE PE	90160036	1000	SINGAPORE PE, REPUBLIC OF SINGAPORE
90110003	1,000	09-May-2022 23:06:57	OAV	ASIA PACIFIC	MALAYSIA	KUALA LUMPUR PE	90110003	1000	KUALA LUMPUR PE, MALAYSIA
92010069	1,000	09-May-2022 23:13:59	OAV	MIDDLE EAST AND AFRICAS	UNITED ARAB EMIRATES	ABU DHABI PE	92010069	1000	ABU DHABI PE, UNITED ARAB EMIRATES
90160019	1,000	09-May-2022 23:17:05	OAV	ASIA PACIFIC	REPUBLIC OF SINGAPORE	SINGAPORE PE	90160019	1000	SINGAPORE PE, REPUBLIC OF SINGAPORE
90110005	1,000	09-May-2022 23:18:54	OAV	ASIA PACIFIC	MALAYSIA	KUALA LUMPUR PE	90110005	1000	KUALA LUMPUR PE, MALAYSIA
92010025	1,000	09-May-2022 23:19:01	OAV	MIDDLE EAST AND AFRICAS	UNITED ARAB EMIRATES	ABU DHABI PE	92010025	1000	ABU DHABI PE, UNITED ARAB EMIRATES
92060028	1,000	09-May-2022 23:20:06	OAV	MIDDLE EAST AND AFRICAS	STATE OF QATAR	DOHA PE	92060028	1000	DOHA PE, STATE OF QATAR
90030109	1,000	09-May-2022 23:38:15	OAV	ASIA PACIFIC	PEOPLES REPUBLIC OF CHINA	MACAU PCG	90030109	1000	MACAU PCG, PEOPLES REPUBLIC OF CHINA
90040005	1,000	09-May-2022 23:36:56	OAV	ASIA PACIFIC	TAIWAN, ROC	TAIPEI MECO	90040005	1000	TAIPEI MECO, TAIWAN, ROC
90030043	1,000	09-May-2022 23:36:59	OAV	ASIA PACIFIC	PEOPLES REPUBLIC OF CHINA	HONGKONG PCG	90030043	1000	HONGKONG PCG, PEOPLES REPUBLIC OF CHINA
90160152	1,000	09-May-2022 23:41:35	OAV	ASIA PACIFIC	REPUBLIC OF SINGAPORE	SINGAPORE PE	90160152	1000	SINGAPORE PE, REPUBLIC OF SINGAPORE
90040006	1,000	09-May-2022 23:48:57	OAV	ASIA PACIFIC	TAIWAN, ROC	TAIPEI MECO	90040006	1000	TAIPEI MECO, TAIWAN, ROC
90030024	1,000	09-May-2022 23:53:00	OAV	ASIA PACIFIC	PEOPLES REPUBLIC OF CHINA	HONGKONG PCG	90030024	1000	HONGKONG PCG, PEOPLES REPUBLIC OF CHINA
90030014	1,000	10-May-2022 00:02:27	OAV	ASIA PACIFIC	PEOPLES REPUBLIC OF CHINA	HONGKONG PCG	90030014	1000	HONGKONG PCG, PEOPLES REPUBLIC OF CHINA
90110006	1,000	10-May-2022 00:04:22	OAV	ASIA PACIFIC	MALAYSIA	KUALA LUMPUR PE	90110006	1000	KUALA LUMPUR PE, MALAYSIA
90040002	1,000	10-May-2022 00:10:33	OAV	ASIA PACIFIC	TAIWAN, ROC	TAIPEI MECO	90040002	1000	TAIPEI MECO, TAIWAN, ROC
92010068	1,000	10-May-2022 00:10:46	OAV	MIDDLE EAST AND AFRICAS	UNITED ARAB EMIRATES	ABU DHABI PE	92010068	1000	ABU DHABI PE, UNITED ARAB EMIRATES
90030034	1,000	10-May-2022 00:10:57	OAV	ASIA PACIFIC	PEOPLES REPUBLIC OF CHINA	HONGKONG PCG	90030034	1000	HONGKONG PCG, PEOPLES REPUBLIC OF CHINA
90040009	1,000	10-May-2022 00:13:14	OAV	ASIA PACIFIC	TAIWAN, ROC	TAIPEI MECO	90040009	1000	TAIPEI MECO, TAIWAN, ROC
92010026	1,000	10-May-2022 00:20:02	OAV	MIDDLE EAST AND AFRICAS	UNITED ARAB EMIRATES	ABU DHABI PE	92010026	1000	ABU DHABI PE, UNITED ARAB EMIRATES
90030110	1,000	10-May-2022 00:20:22	OAV	ASIA PACIFIC	PEOPLES REPUBLIC OF CHINA	MACAU PCG	90030110	1000	MACAU PCG, PEOPLES REPUBLIC OF CHINA
90040008	1,000	10-May-2022 00:33:59	OAV	ASIA PACIFIC	TAIWAN, ROC	TAIPEI MECO	90040008	1000	TAIPEI MECO, TAIWAN, ROC
90040011	1,000	10-May-2022 00:36:34	OAV	ASIA PACIFIC	TAIWAN, ROC	TAIPEI MECO	90040011	1000	TAIPEI MECO, TAIWAN, ROC
90030064	1,000	10-May-2022 00:39:17	OAV	ASIA PACIFIC	PEOPLES REPUBLIC OF CHINA	HONGKONG PCG	90030064	1000	HONGKONG PCG, PEOPLES REPUBLIC OF CHINA
90040010	1,000	10-May-2022 00:43:34	OAV	ASIA PACIFIC	TAIWAN, ROC	TAIPEI MECO	90040010	1000	TAIPEI MECO, TAIWAN, ROC
90030025	1,000	10-May-2022 00:46:37	OAV	ASIA PACIFIC	PEOPLES REPUBLIC OF CHINA	HONGKONG PCG	90030025	1000	HONGKONG PCG, PEOPLES REPUBLIC OF CHINA
90030015	1,000	10-May-2022 01:13:10	OAV	ASIA PACIFIC	PEOPLES REPUBLIC OF CHINA	HONGKONG PCG	90030015	1000	HONGKONG PCG, PEOPLES REPUBLIC OF CHINA
90030111	1,000	10-May-2022 01:14:38	OAV	ASIA PACIFIC	PEOPLES REPUBLIC OF CHINA	MACAU PCG	90030111	1000	MACAU PCG, PEOPLES REPUBLIC OF CHINA
93100002	1,000	10-May-2022 01:24:53	OAV	EUROPE	KINGDOM OF SPAIN	MADRID PE	93100002	1000	MADRID PE, KINGDOM OF SPAIN
90030045	1,000	10-May-2022 01:26:07	OAV	ASIA PACIFIC	PEOPLES REPUBLIC OF CHINA	HONGKONG PCG	90030045	1000	HONGKONG PCG, PEOPLES REPUBLIC OF CHINA
90030028	1,000	10-May-2022 01:39:33	OAV	ASIA PACIFIC	PEOPLES REPUBLIC OF CHINA	HONGKONG PCG	90030028	1000	HONGKONG PCG, PEOPLES REPUBLIC OF CHINA
90160002	1,000	10-May-2022 01:56:04	OAV	ASIA PACIFIC	REPUBLIC OF SINGAPORE	SINGAPORE PE	90160002	1000	SINGAPORE PE, REPUBLIC OF SINGAPORE
92010108	1,000	10-May-2022 01:56:45	OAV	MIDDLE EAST AND AFRICAS	UNITED ARAB EMIRATES	DUBAI PCG	92010108	1000	DUBAI PCG, UNITED ARAB EMIRATES
90030031	1,000	10-May-2022 02:00:07	OAV	ASIA PACIFIC	PEOPLES REPUBLIC OF CHINA	HONGKONG PCG	90030031	1000	HONGKONG PCG, PEOPLES REPUBLIC OF CHINA
92010262	1,000	10-May-2022 02:02:57	OAV	MIDDLE EAST AND AFRICAS	UNITED ARAB EMIRATES	DUBAI PCG	92010262	1000	DUBAI PCG, UNITED ARAB EMIRATES
92010103	1,000	10-May-2022 02:05:05	OAV	MIDDLE EAST AND AFRICAS	UNITED ARAB EMIRATES	DUBAI PCG	92010103	1000	DUBAI PCG, UNITED ARAB EMIRATES
90030112	1,000	10-May-2022 02:08:05	OAV	ASIA PACIFIC	PEOPLES REPUBLIC OF CHINA	MACAU PCG	90030112	1000	MACAU PCG, PEOPLES REPUBLIC OF CHINA

CLUSTERED	ACTUAL	RECEPTIONDATETIME	REGION	PROVINCE	MUNICIPALITY	BARANGAY	PRECINCT_ID	CLUSTERTOTAL	POLLINGCENTER
92810233	1,300	10-May-2022 02:07:38	OAV	MIDDLE EAST AND AFRICAS	UNITED ARAB EMIRATES	DUBAI PCG	92810233	1000	DUBAI PCG, UNITED ARAB EMIRATES
92810102	1,000	10-May-2022 02:09:51	OAV	MIDDLE EAST AND AFRICAS	UNITED ARAB EMIRATES	DUBAI PCG	92810102	1000	DUBAI PCG, UNITED ARAB EMIRATES
92810115	1,000	10-May-2022 02:11:60	OAV	MIDDLE EAST AND AFRICAS	UNITED ARAB EMIRATES	DUBAI PCG	92810115	1000	DUBAI PCG, UNITED ARAB EMIRATES
92810189	1,000	10-May-2022 07:17:41	OAV	MIDDLE EAST AND AFRICAS	UNITED ARAB EMIRATES	DUBAI PCG	92810189	1000	DUBAI PCG, UNITED ARAB EMIRATES
92060004	1,000	10-May-2022 02:25:14	OAV	MIDDLE EAST AND AFRICAS	STATE OF QATAR	DOHA PE	92060004	1000	DOHA PE, STATE OF QATAR
93100004	1,500	10-May-2022 07:27:33	OAV	EUROPE	KINGDOM OF SPAIN	MADRID PE	93100003	1000	MADRID PE, KINGDOM OF SPAIN
90030046	1,200	10-May-2022 02:28:31	OAV	ASIA PACIFIC	PEOPLES REPUBLIC OF CHINA	HONGKONG PCG	90030046	1000	HONGKONG PCG, PEOPLES REPUBLIC OF CHINA
92090005	1,000	10-May-2022 02:49:59	OAV	MIDDLE EAST AND AFRICAS	SULTANATE OF OMAN	MUSCAT PE	92090005	1000	MUSCAT PE, SULTANATE OF OMAN
90160023	1,000	10-May-2022 02:49:10	OAV	ASIA PACIFIC	REPUBLIC OF SINGAPORE	SINGAPORE PE	90160023	1000	SINGAPORE PE, REPUBLIC OF SINGAPORE
93100004	1,000	10-May-2022 02:52:25	OAV	EUROPE	KINGDOM OF SPAIN	MADRID PE	93100004	1000	MADRID PE, KINGDOM OF SPAIN
92090007	1,000	10-May-2022 02:56:18	OAV	MIDDLE EAST AND AFRICAS	SULTANATE OF OMAN	MUSCAT PE	92090007	1000	MUSCAT PE, SULTANATE OF OMAN
90030066	1,000	10-May-2022 02:59:41	OAV	ASIA PACIFIC	PEOPLES REPUBLIC OF CHINA	HONGKONG PCG	90030066	1000	HONGKONG PCG, PEOPLES REPUBLIC OF CHINA
90090113	1,000	10-May-2022 03:01:17	OAV	ASIA PACIFIC	PEOPLES REPUBLIC OF CHINA	MACAU PCG	90090113	1000	MACAU PCG, PEOPLES REPUBLIC OF CHINA
90160072	1,000	10-May-2022 03:02:33	OAV	ASIA PACIFIC	REPUBLIC OF SINGAPORE	SINGAPORE PE	90160072	1000	SINGAPORE PE, REPUBLIC OF SINGAPORE
92060015	1,000	10-May-2022 03:18:34	OAV	MIDDLE EAST AND AFRICAS	STATE OF QATAR	DOHA PE	92060015	1000	DOHA PE, STATE OF QATAR
90030017	1,000	10-May-2022 03:24:45	OAV	ASIA PACIFIC	PEOPLES REPUBLIC OF CHINA	HONGKONG PCG	90030017	1000	HONGKONG PCG, PEOPLES REPUBLIC OF CHINA
90160024	1,000	10-May-2022 03:40:37	OAV	ASIA PACIFIC	REPUBLIC OF SINGAPORE	SINGAPORE PE	90160024	1000	SINGAPORE PE, REPUBLIC OF SINGAPORE
92120250	1,000	10-May-2022 03:44:11	OAV	MIDDLE EAST AND AFRICAS	KINGDOM OF SAUDI ARABIA	POLO AL KHOBAR	92120250	1000	POLO AL KHOBAR, KINGDOM OF SAUDI ARABIA (RIYADH)
92120269	1,000	10-May-2022 03:47:33	OAV	MIDDLE EAST AND AFRICAS	KINGDOM OF SAUDI ARABIA	POLO AL KHOBAR	92120269	1000	POLO AL KHOBAR, KINGDOM OF SAUDI ARABIA (RIYADH)
92120233	1,000	10-May-2022 03:49:33	OAV	MIDDLE EAST AND AFRICAS	KINGDOM OF SAUDI ARABIA	POLO AL KHOBAR	92120233	1000	POLO AL KHOBAR, KINGDOM OF SAUDI ARABIA (RIYADH)
90080114	1,000	10-May-2022 03:53:27	OAV	ASIA PACIFIC	PEOPLES REPUBLIC OF CHINA	MACAU PCG	90080114	1000	MACAU PCG, PEOPLES REPUBLIC OF CHINA
93100021	1,000	10-May-2022 03:59:36	OAV	EUROPE	KINGDOM OF SPAIN	BARCELONA PCG	93100021	1000	BARCELONA PCG, KINGDOM OF SPAIN
92120270	1,000	10-May-2022 04:15:47	OAV	MIDDLE EAST AND AFRICAS	KINGDOM OF SAUDI ARABIA	POLO AL KHOBAR	92120270	1000	POLO AL KHOBAR, KINGDOM OF SAUDI ARABIA (RIYADH)
90160025	1,000	10-May-2022 04:36:06	OAV	ASIA PACIFIC	REPUBLIC OF SINGAPORE	SINGAPORE PE	90160025	1000	SINGAPORE PE, REPUBLIC OF SINGAPORE
92140234	1,000	10-May-2022 04:45:48	OAV	MIDDLE EAST AND AFRICAS	KINGDOM OF SAUDI ARABIA	POLO AL KHOBAR	92120214	1000	POLO AL KHOBAR, KINGDOM OF SAUDI ARABIA (RIYADH)
90160074	1,000	10-May-2022 05:01:28	OAV	ASIA PACIFIC	REPUBLIC OF SINGAPORE	SINGAPORE PE	90160074	1000	SINGAPORE PE, REPUBLIC OF SINGAPORE
92120251	1,000	10-May-2022 05:27:17	OAV	MIDDLE EAST AND AFRICAS	KINGDOM OF SAUDI ARABIA	POLO AL KHOBAR	92120252	1000	POLO AL KHOBAR, KINGDOM OF SAUDI ARABIA (RIYADH)
93100020	1,000	10-May-2022 05:42:05	OAV	EUROPE	KINGDOM OF SPAIN	BARCELONA PCG	93100020	1000	BARCELONA PCG, KINGDOM OF SPAIN
90160076	1,000	10-May-2022 05:58:23	OAV	ASIA PACIFIC	REPUBLIC OF SINGAPORE	SINGAPORE PE	90160076	1000	SINGAPORE PE, REPUBLIC OF SINGAPORE
90160059	1,000	10-May-2022 06:00:57	OAV	ASIA PACIFIC	REPUBLIC OF SINGAPORE	SINGAPORE PE	90160059	1000	SINGAPORE PE, REPUBLIC OF SINGAPORE
90160013	1,000	10-May-2022 06:13:06	OAV	ASIA PACIFIC	REPUBLIC OF SINGAPORE	SINGAPORE PE	90160013	1000	SINGAPORE PE, REPUBLIC OF SINGAPORE
90160027	1,000	10-May-2022 06:29:15	OAV	ASIA PACIFIC	REPUBLIC OF SINGAPORE	SINGAPORE PE	90160027	1000	SINGAPORE PE, REPUBLIC OF SINGAPORE
90160042	1,000	10-May-2022 06:31:05	OAV	ASIA PACIFIC	REPUBLIC OF SINGAPORE	SINGAPORE PE	90160042	1000	SINGAPORE PE, REPUBLIC OF SINGAPORE
93100019	1,000	10-May-2022 06:42:31	OAV	EUROPE	KINGDOM OF SPAIN	BARCELONA PCG	93100019	1000	BARCELONA PCG, KINGDOM OF SPAIN
90160043	1,000	10-May-2022 07:06:50	OAV	ASIA PACIFIC	REPUBLIC OF SINGAPORE	SINGAPORE PE	90160043	1000	SINGAPORE PE, REPUBLIC OF SINGAPORE
92080008	1,000	10-May-2022 07:37:38	OAV	MIDDLE EAST AND AFRICAS	KINGDOM OF BAHRAIN	MANAMA PE	92080008	1000	MANAMA PE, KINGDOM OF BAHRAIN
92080002	1,000	10-May-2022 16:31:34	OAV	MIDDLE EAST AND AFRICAS	KINGDOM OF BAHRAIN	MANAMA PE	92080002	1000	MANAMA PE, KINGDOM OF BAHRAIN
92080006	1,000	10-May-2022 16:34:45	OAV	MIDDLE EAST AND AFRICAS	KINGDOM OF BAHRAIN	MANAMA PE	92080006	1000	MANAMA PE, KINGDOM OF BAHRAIN
92080010	1,000	10-May-2022 16:35:46	OAV	MIDDLE EAST AND AFRICAS	KINGDOM OF BAHRAIN	MANAMA PE	92080010	1000	MANAMA PE, KINGDOM OF BAHRAIN
92080012	1,000	10-May-2022 16:37:19	OAV	MIDDLE EAST AND AFRICAS	KINGDOM OF BAHRAIN	MANAMA PE	92080012	1000	MANAMA PE, KINGDOM OF BAHRAIN
92080004	1,000	10-May-2022 16:51:37	OAV	MIDDLE EAST AND AFRICAS	KINGDOM OF BAHRAIN	MANAMA PE	92080004	1000	MANAMA PE, KINGDOM OF BAHRAIN
92060030	1,000	10-May-2022 22:27:56	OAV	MIDDLE EAST AND AFRICAS	STATE OF QATAR	DOHA PE	92060030	1000	DOHA PE, STATE OF QATAR
92060005	1,000	10-May-2022 23:39:17	OAV	MIDDLE EAST AND AFRICAS	STATE OF QATAR	DOHA PE	92060005	1000	DOHA PE, STATE OF QATAR
92060016	1,000	10-May-2022 23:48:28	OAV	MIDDLE EAST AND AFRICAS	STATE OF QATAR	DOHA PE	92060016	1000	DOHA PE, STATE OF QATAR
92060031	1,000	10-May-2022 23:59:38	OAV	MIDDLE EAST AND AFRICAS	STATE OF QATAR	DOHA PE	92060031	1000	DOHA PE, STATE OF QATAR
92060006	1,000	11-May-2022 00:43:18	OAV	MIDDLE EAST AND AFRICAS	STATE OF QATAR	DOHA PE	92060006	1000	DOHA PE, STATE OF QATAR
92060012	1,000	11-May-2022 01:47:05	OAV	MIDDLE EAST AND AFRICAS	STATE OF QATAR	DOHA PE	92060012	1000	DOHA PE, STATE OF QATAR
92060017	1,000	11-May-2022 02:02:02	OAV	MIDDLE EAST AND AFRICAS	STATE OF QATAR	DOHA PE	92060017	1000	DOHA PE, STATE OF QATAR
92060007	1,000	11-May-2022 02:12:15	OAV	MIDDLE EAST AND AFRICAS	STATE OF QATAR	DOHA PE	92060007	1000	DOHA PE, STATE OF QATAR
92060008	1,000	11-May-2022 03:13:46	OAV	MIDDLE EAST AND AFRICAS	STATE OF QATAR	DOHA PE	92060008	1000	DOHA PE, STATE OF QATAR
92060034	1,000	11-May-2022 05:17:19	OAV	MIDDLE EAST AND AFRICAS	STATE OF QATAR	DOHA PE	92060034	1000	DOHA PE, STATE OF QATAR
92060033	1,000	11-May-2022 05:23:13	OAV	MIDDLE EAST AND AFRICAS	STATE OF QATAR	DOHA PE	92060033	1000	DOHA PE, STATE OF QATAR
92060019	1,000	11-May-2022 05:53:58	OAV	MIDDLE EAST AND AFRICAS	STATE OF QATAR	DOHA PE	92060019	1000	DOHA PE, STATE OF QATAR
92120253	1,000	11-May-2022 17:19:39	OAV	MIDDLE EAST AND AFRICAS	KINGDOM OF SAUDI ARABIA	POLO AL KHOBAR	92120253	1000	POLO AL KHOBAR, KINGDOM OF SAUDI ARABIA (RIYADH)
92120230	1,000	11-May-2022 17:21:34	OAV	MIDDLE EAST AND AFRICAS	KINGDOM OF SAUDI ARABIA	POLO AL KHOBAR	92120230	1000	POLO AL KHOBAR, KINGDOM OF SAUDI ARABIA (RIYADH)
92120232	1,000	11-May-2022 17:23:09	OAV	MIDDLE EAST AND AFRICAS	KINGDOM OF SAUDI ARABIA	POLO AL KHOBAR	92120232	1000	POLO AL KHOBAR, KINGDOM OF SAUDI ARABIA (RIYADH)

28
Constant Prayer – Franklin Ysaac – May 17, 2023

Nung Mayo 9, nagtapos ang ating novena Kay San Jose!

Sa harap ng Imahen ni Santa Maria de la Imaculada Concepcion sa Manila Cathedral, nag Rosaryo at Nag novena mga kasama natin sa pangunguna ni Sister Teresita Elevera ng Franciscan Sisters of Mary.

Salamat sa mga dumalo sa simbahan at katulad ng sinabi natin, ang milagro ay sa huli.

Meron po nilabas ang Comelec na Hindi mag tugma ang election results sa transmission logs. Obvious na May milagro ginawa sa totoong resulta at nagpatunay na Hindi makatotoo ang buong pangyayaring eleksyon .

Ngayon, sa tulong ng ating abogado,maghain tayo uli ng supplemental sa korte Suprema para mag paliwanag sa iregularidad ang comelec para malaman ng taumbayan ang malaking pag babaliktad ng resulta .

At para Mas mapatunayan na Hindi totoo, maghahain uli ng supplemental petition na ilabas na ng telco ang CDRs na magpapatunay na Meron o walang ganun 20M plus transmisssion nung unang Oras mula Alas Siete hanggang alas otso. Pag walang transmission sa palagay namin, tunay na Yung transmission ay ginawang milagro .

Abangan po natin etong supplemental at malapit na rin tayo sa katotohanan.

Hindi po talaga natutulog ang Diyos at ang kanyang Ina na sumasaklolo parati sa mga hiling at dasal ng buong sambayanan.

Maraming Salamat po O Diyos na matulungin at maawain.

Mahal namin Mama Mary, Maraming Salamat sa pag gabay niyo po sa amin.

Huwag po kayong magsawa na tumulong at mag milagro po sa mga taga sunod po sa utos ng Inyong Anak na si Hesus.

Abangan po namin na Sana matapos na rin ang kalbaryo namin na ngayon isang taon na naghirap at nakaranas ng kahirapan .

Marami pa susunod kami hihilingin sa Inyo po at pag sinagot na mga supplemental petition namin Giginhawa na rin ang pakiramdam ng taumbayan .

Amen .

(Translation)

Last May 9, our novena to San Jose ended!

In front of the Image of Santa Maria de la Immaculada Concepcion in Manila Cathedral, our companions did Rosary and Novena led by Sister Teresita Elevera of Franciscan Sisters of Mary.

Thanks to those who attended the church and as we said the miracle was at the end.

Comelec released something that the election results do not match with the transmission logs. Obviously there is a miracle done in the real result and proved that the whole election event is not true.

Now, with the help of our lawyer, let's file a supplementary file again to the Supreme Court to explain the irregularity of the comelec so that the people will know the big reversal of the results.

And to prove that it is not true, telco will again file a supplemental petition that will prove that there is or does not have that 20M plus transmission in the first hour from seven to eight o'clock. If there is no transmission in our opinion, it is true that the transmission was made a miracle.

Let's wait for this supplemental and we are also close to the truth.

God and His Mother never sleeps who always helps the wishes and prayers of the whole congregation.

Thank you very much, O God who is helpful and merciful.

Our beloved Mama Mary, Thank you very much for guiding us.

Don't get tired of helping and doing miracles to the followers of Your Son Jesus.

Let's wait for the Calvary that has been suffering for a year and experienced hardship will finally end.

More will follow, we will ask from you and when our supplemental petitions are answered, the feeling of the countrymen will be relieved.

Amen .

• •

29
1,241,898 VOTES
DISENFRANCHISED ??? –
Ronnie Adriano Amoroso

SAGOTIN MO, EXPLAIN MO ETO COMELEC !!!
PRECINCTS with NO E.R. TRANSMITTED FROM
VCM.

AUDIT FINDING COMPILED BY MS. LHOT AGUILAR, 4/27/2023:	

# of LOCAL PRECINCTS with NO E.R.	1,143
# of REGISTERED VOTERS	694,837

# of OVERSEAS PRECINCTS with NO E.R.	620
# of REGISTERED VOTERS	547,061

QUESTION: 1,241,898 VOTES DISENFRANCHISED ???

SAGOTIN MO, EXPLAIN MO ETO COMELEC !!!

1,241,898 VOTES DISENFRANCHISED ???

SAGOTIN MO, EXPLAIN MO ETO COMELEC !!!

PRECINCTS with NO E.R. TRANSMITTED FROM VCM.

. . . .

30
Thank you Tina Astorga and USA folks – Franklin Ysaac – May 17, 2023

Maraming Salamat Mam Tina Astorga sa mga explanation ng katulad po niyo na kahit na sa America kayo malakas ang boses ng mga kababayan natin na tugisin ang katiwalian.

At sa Inyong panawagan sa mga politika na sa ngayon at tahimik Sana purima sila sa People's Mandamus para ma iparating sa kinauukulan na sagutin ang karapatan na malaman ng taumbayan Bakit tinatago ang hinihiling ng TNTrio mandamus at People's Mandamus .

Siguro bansagan natin ang version ng comelec ang Ibig sabihin ng TNT ay TAGO NG TAGO.

Kaya ang apela ng mga Pilipino sa amerika palakasin natin ang pag pirma sa Peope's Mandamus para malaman ng taumbayan at sa mundo na ang nakasulat sa mandato ng comelec charter ay TRUTH AND TRANSPARENCY at HINDI TAGO NG TAGO.

Mabuhay po kayo Mam Tina at sa mga Pilipino sa Amerika at sa mga Pilipino sa buong mundo.

Thank you very much Mam Tina Astorga for the explanations of people like you that even though you are in America, our countrymen have a strong voice to fight corruption.

And in your appeal to the politicians who are silent for now, I hope they will clean the People's Mandamus so that they will be brought to the authority to answer the right of the people to know Why are the requests of TNTrio Mandamus and People's Mandatus hidden.

Maybe we will destroy the version of the COMELEC which means TNT is always HIDDEN.

So the appeal of Filipinos to America is to strengthen the signing of the People's Mandamus so that the people and the world will know that what is written in the mandate of the COMELEC Charter is TRUTH AND TRANSPARENCY and NOT HIDDEN.

Mabuhay po kayo Mam Tina and to Filipinos in America and to Filipinos around the world.

Translation

Thank you very much Mam Tina Astorga for the explanations of people like you that even though you are in America, our countrymen have a strong voice to fight corruption.

And in your appeal to the politicians who are silent for now, I hope they will clean the People's Mandamus so that they will be brought to the authority to answer the right of the people to know Why are the requests of TNTrio Mandamus and People's Mandatus hidden.

Maybe we will destroy the version of the COMELEC which means TNT is always HIDDEN.

So the appeal of Filipinos to America is to strengthen the signing of the People's Mandamus so that the people and the world will know that what is written in the mandate of the COMELEC Charter is TRUTH AND TRANSPARENCY and NOT HIDDEN.

Mabuhay po kayo Mam Tina and to Filipinos in America and to Filipinos around the world.

. . . . .

31
Posters by Supporters

Franklin Ysaac
4h · 🌐

TNTrio's mission is done ! Now it's the presidential bet's turn to finish what was unfinished!

The truth is out! Calling on presidential bet to issue statement of support to people's mandamus! Million followers await you!

Google Trends predict a Robredo win

GOOGLE TREND REPORT

Covering from February 5 to March 2, 2022

BREAKDOWN OF SCORES OF THE TWO CANDIDATES IN THE VARIOUS REGIONS OF THE COUNTRY:

REGION	ROBREDO	MARCOS JR.
METRO MANILA	59	41
CALABARZON	61	39
CENTRAL LUZON	57	43
CENTRAL VISAYAS	56	44
ILOCOS REGION	48	52
CAR	60	40
CARAGA	68	32
CAGAYAN VALLEY	54	46
BICOL	69	32
W. VISAYAS	61	39
E. VISAYAS	55	45
C.VISAYAS	56	44
NORTHERN MINDANAO	58	42
DAVAO REGION	53	47
ZAMBOANGA PENINSULA	59	41
SOCCSKARGEN	59	41
NIMAROPA	58	42

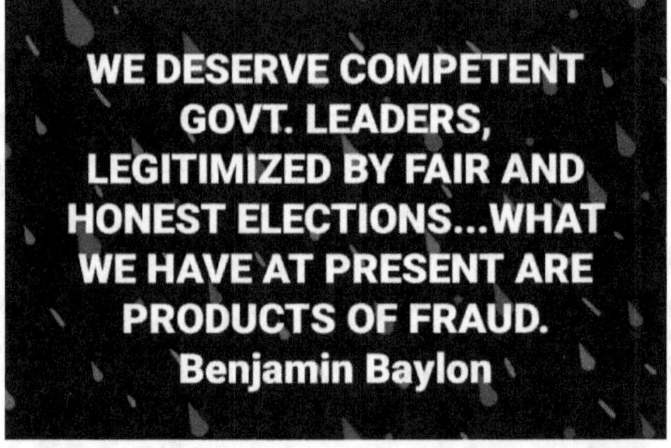
Cornered, the respondents, outside the court, pour optics, sound bytes, and empty rhetorics!Just swear in court!

WE DESERVE COMPETENT GOVT. LEADERS, LEGITIMIZED BY FAIR AND HONEST ELECTIONS...WHAT WE HAVE AT PRESENT ARE PRODUCTS OF FRAUD.
Benjamin Baylon

We gave them every single chance to tell the whole truth and they failed! Now, it's time for wrath of God to befall on them!

Al Leon - DUTERTE'S COMELEC #PHelection2022

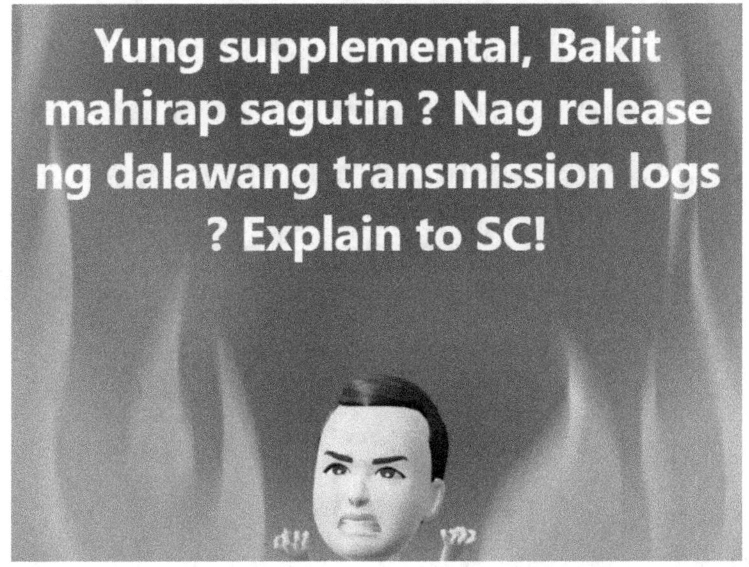

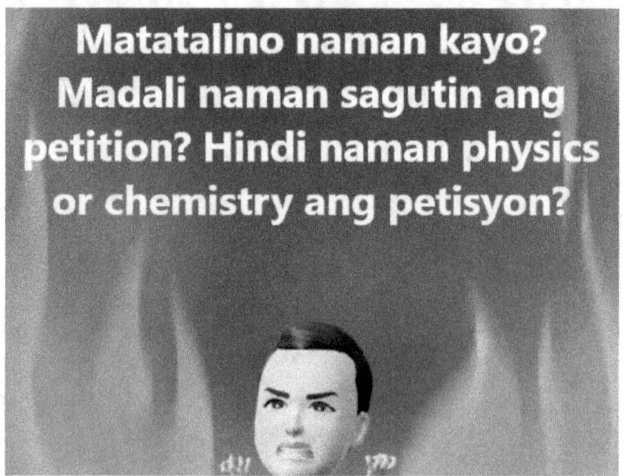
If you don't agree with the truth, does that make you an accomplice to the lies? Then you become one of the ACCOMPLIES!!!
Bakit nauna ER time stamp sa Transmission log? Saan Pumunta ang transmission ng ER? Paging telco?
Matatalino naman kayo? Madali naman sagutin ang petition? Hindi naman physics or chemistry ang petisyon?

Our lawyers' hands will be full and their time occupied as respondents commit blunder after blunder!

Solgen, govt defender, responded to SC: Delay and More Delay! Telcos, Smartmatic:No response, defying SC order! Action time now

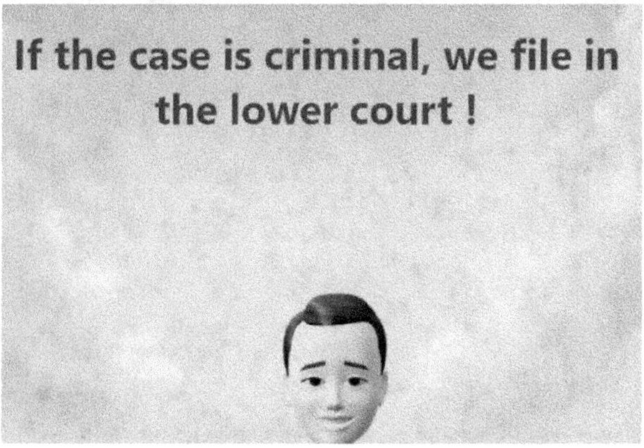

If the case is criminal, we file in the lower court !

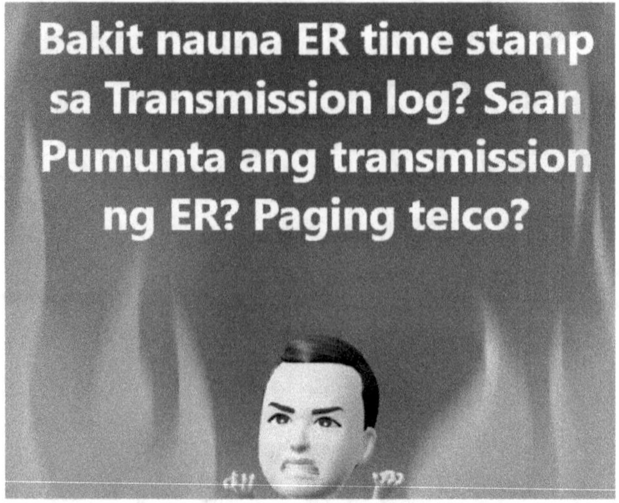
Bakit nauna ER time stamp sa Transmission log? Saan Pumunta ang transmission ng ER? Paging telco?

After our novena which will end on May 9, the day of reckoning, we will make another for release of Sen Leila!

OCTA Research: "8 in ten Filipinos believe the country was moving in the right direction. " If they can steal elections, they can rig surveys!

Reason we filed mandamus before SC is the case is a constitutional case! Only SC,as highest body, can decide!

If the case is administrative, we file in the ombudsman !

In court cases, there are no second takes! You study and prepare your case and opponent's before every hearing !

The battle for truth will be shifting to legal court as respondents are suffering from.....

It pays to have the best and experienced legal minds!That's our cutting edge!

SC cannot dismiss mandamus because it's a constitutional case! That's the constitutional right of every Filipino !

In legal cases, we listen to top lawyers strategize and counter strategize like in a moot court!

Like in a debate, you look for your opponent's weakest link and demolish his premises!That's how you win!

Nanay ko: wag ka sinungaling!Mabigat yan! Sabihin mo totoo, gagaan loob mo, tahimik buhay mo, at sarap tulog mo!

If you are one BRAVE HEART
join the Fight for truth! It will
be a long fight but we will not
stop till we win! To thy
kingdom come!

The war of truth has begun!
Comelec says transmission
logs is perfect and unassailable
! We proved them wrong!

" Day of Reckoning " is May 9!
Join the thousands and make
our presence felt that they are
not above the law!

Hindi paninira ang pagsasabi ng totoo. Lalo na kung pilit kang nililinlang at nililito. Walang MAGNANAKAW na nagmamahal sa kapwa. Walang MAGNANAKAW na nagmamahal sa bansa.

1:38 AM · 04 May 23 · **220** Views

The respondents have been stonewalling!The Good Lord has laid the stone that has become the cornerstone of the Truth!

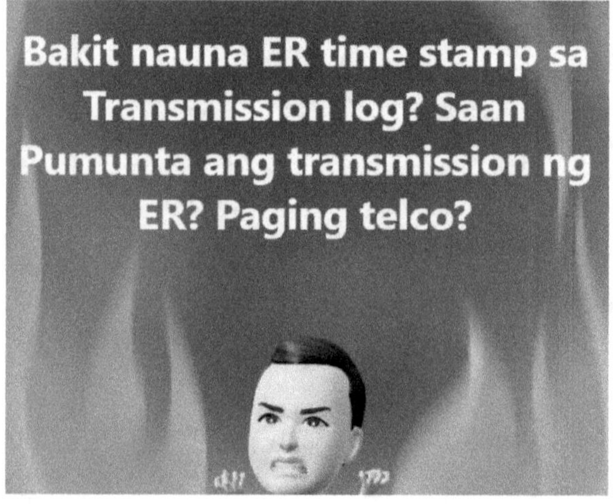
Truth has only one face ! Lies have many faces and they cannot even face the truth !

Learned from our lawyer about hostile witness in the event cases are filed against responsible or irresponsible officials!

Bakit nauna ER time stamp sa Transmission log? Saan Pumunta ang transmission ng ER? Paging telco?

TNTrio
Wake up call May
9, 2023,
in comelec
PRAYER VIGIL
is a Peaceful
Poeple Power...

VP Leni: "You are what you tolerate." If a rigged election does not fill you with moral outrage, you become what you tolerate.

Dear GOD
please protect and
guide the TNTrio
and those fighting
for the Truths..

"2ND PAMPANGA BATAAN MARCH TO COMELEC"
Ika-unang Anibersaryo
ARAW NG PANDARAYA AT PANDURUGAS
Mayo 9, 2022
8AM
Aimee F. Ampoloquio
Socorro B. Inting
BBM
George Garcia
Marlon Casquejo
Rey E. Bulay
ILABAS ANG TRANSMISSION LOGS NOW! NOT "DECEPTION" LOGS! COMELEC /GLOBE/ SMART/DITO
TRUTH RULES!
NO TO SMARTMATIC!
YES TO HYBRID!
ELECTORAL REFORM!
SAVE DEMOCRACY!
FOLLOW CONSTITUTION/ RULE OF LAW!
FRED SANTOS

When you are on the right path, you take the offensive and let the opponent commit more mistakes!

Mila Alvarez Magno: "AN OPEN LETTER TO VP LENI ROBREDO: "Being one of your very many supporters, please allow me to dare make an observation and suggestion to you. ¶

1 Your silence in the wake of the Mandamus petition of the TNTrio has baffled and confused many of your supporters. They understood why you initially accepted the proclamation of Marcos and Sara. However, after your period of foreign speaking engagements and Angat Buhay projects, they now look to you for leadership and support in the efforts of the TNTrio and others to show that the election was rigged. ¶

2 Please communicate with Gen Eliseo Rio and the TNTrio to understand what they are working hard to achieve against all odds and somehow show the people that you support their efforts to LEARN THE TRUTH. Your supporters and even the Liberal Party are now rudderless and many have lost heart for the fight for true justice and democracy in the Philippines. Many are puzzled by your silence and have even wondered whether you are truly the leader we had all hoped for. Some have even spoken about giving up the fight and not voting in the next elections because it would be useless in the face of a biased COMELEC. Where once hundreds of thousands and even millions rallied to your side, now not even 25 thousand have signed an online petition supporting the Mandamus petition. ¶

Please come out once again and lead the people who are crying for justice and true democracy for our country. At this time, no other person exists who can do what ONLY YOU CAN. That is, to UNITE us once again. The country is crying out for your leadership. PLEASE LEAD US NOW. ¶

~ Fred Cyd Gallardo ¶   *Panawagan!*

To ALL KAKAMPINKS: FOLLOW and READ ** FRANKLIN YSAAC **

HE AND HIS TEAM ARE FIGHTING FOR THE TRUTH ABOUT THE ELECTION RESULTS TO COME OUT

Kung kayo ay matitinong Pilipino at isang tao mayroon sariling pag-iisip magtatanong kayo - (1) "Bakit nanahimik sina LENI ROBREDO tungkol sa DAYAAN?" .... (2) "Bakit? parati siyang magpaliwaliw sa labas ng bansa?".. (3) " Bakit? binigyan ba siya ng yaman (MARCOS Gold) PATAGO LANG upang (a) manahimik na lang at (b) magbabyahi na lang parati sa labas ng Pilipinas.

May O9 2023
1st Anniversary "ARAW NG PANDARAYA"
Magandang umaga po!
— with Nelson Samillano.

HAPPY 1st NATIONAL
DAYAAN DAY!!

exclusive to pulangaws only.

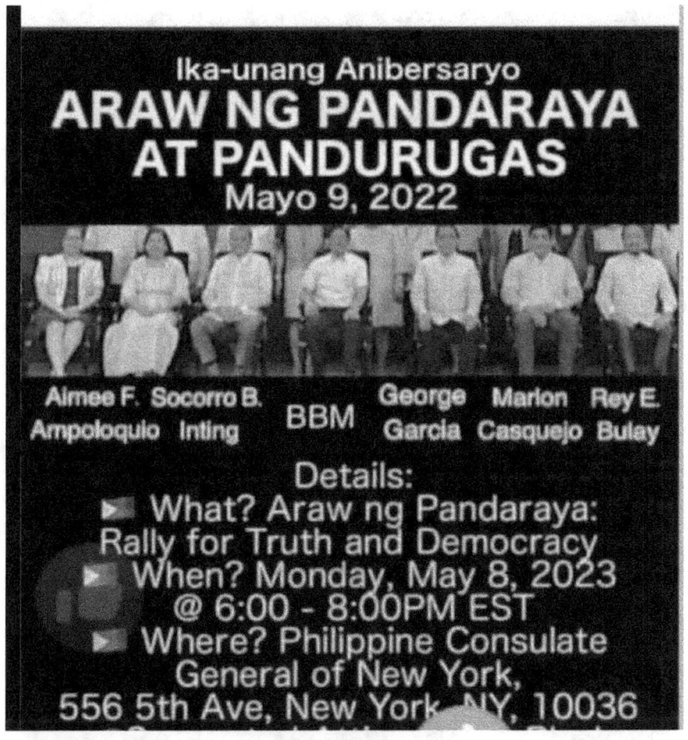
Ika-unang Anibersaryo
ARAW NG PANDARAYA
AT PANDURUGAS
Mayo 9, 2022
Aimee F. Ampoloquio
Socorro B. Inting
BBM
George Garcia
Marlon Casquejo
Rey E. Bulay
Details:
What? Araw ng Pandaraya:
Rally for Truth and Democracy
When? Monday, May 8, 2023
@ 6:00 - 8:00PM EST
Where? Philippine Consulate
General of New York,
556 5th Ave, New York, NY, 10036

1986 DINAYA
Pag-walkout ng tinaguriang
'Comelec 35' sa snap elections, isa
sa mga mitsa ng 1986 EDSA
Revolution
GMA Integrated News   Follow
Eliseo Rio Jr
Thu at 10:39 PM
Proof beyond reasonable doubt that the 2022
Election was rigged.
2022 DINAYA
The evidence is overwhelming that the
national election is failed clearly, the people
of the Philippines Marcos, Jr. and Sarah
Duterte were not elected legitimately.
Lee Rhiannon
PROOF BEYOND
REASONABLE DOUBT
Tell your opposition leaders

The TELCOS' Call Detail
Records (CDRs) would show
that there were almost no VCM
transmissions thru their
networks in the 1st hour.

When regulators commit
irregularities, they become
IRREGULATORS!

COMELEC NANLOKO!
Reception Logs
ang binigay, HINDI
Transmission Logs!

ABOGADO NA
DOKTOR PA!?

TNTrio MANDAMUS Petition

General Eliseo Rio, Jr. (R)

Speak the
truth, even if
your voice
shakes

WE WANT
YOU!
TO FIGHT FOR
OUR COUNTRY!

#SupportTNTrio

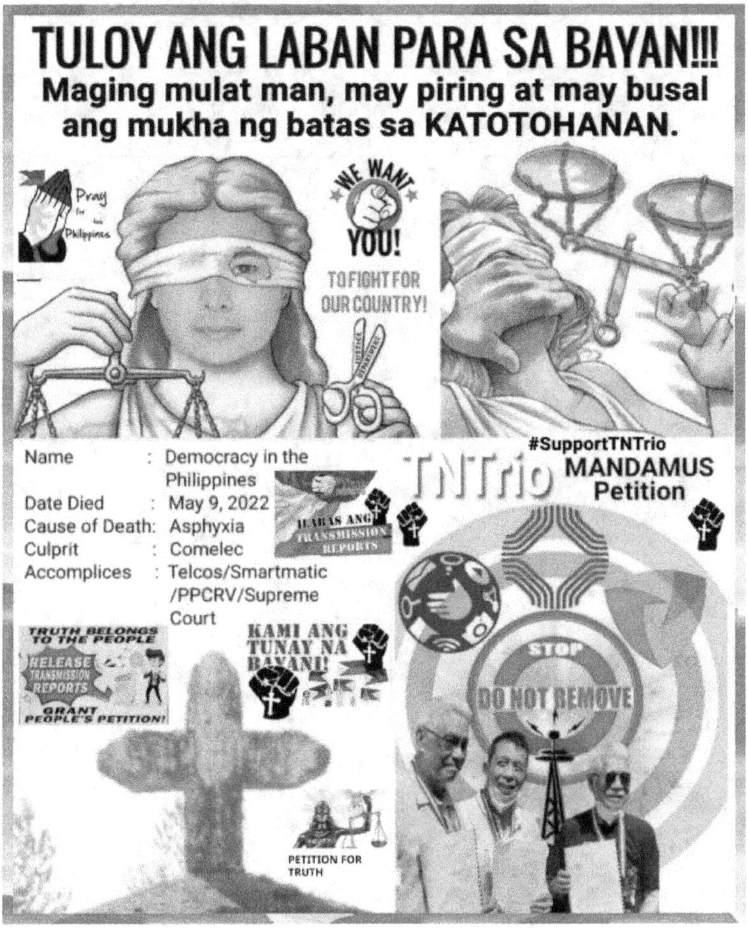

TULOY ANG LABAN PARA SA BAYAN!!!

Maging mulat man, may piring at may busal ang mukha ng batas sa KATOTOHANAN.

IMPEACH THE
ENTIRE COMELEC
BETRAYAL OF
PUBLIC TRUST

Bakit pa mag eeleksyon!!!
Kung dadayain lang din
naman at ang npupuwesto ay
yung mga magnanakaw!!!
Wag na magbotohan!!! Dapat
tanggalin na ang
comelecta !!!

May 9, 2022 - i mourn the
day Comelec in cahoots with
SmartMagic disenfranchised
millions of Filipino voters.

The TNTrio at their late 70s are still fighting for the nation at the risk of their safety. But where are our Filipino youth?

Tina A. Astorga
4d · 🌐

I am a feminist. I fight for equity for women on all levels. I fight against domestic violence and abuse of children. Feminism is founded on justice!

Tina A. Astorga
3d · 🌐

Let us not allow the election fraud to be just another news that would pass away. Let us keep the issue burning till Comelec get SCALDED!

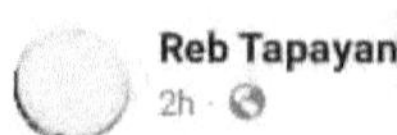

https://m.facebook.com/story.php?story_fbid=10226359102657023&i
=1026127023&mibextid=Nif5oz

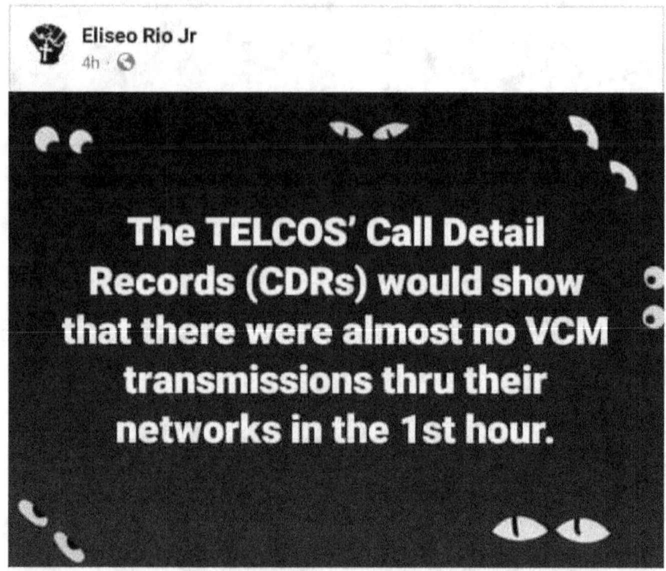

The TRUTH on the real outcome of the May 2022 election will set the PH free. Showing the transmission log is the KEY.

When my kids asked why I haven't given up yet, I replied" This is for you, keeping our country safe from these wreckers!"

The truth is out! Calling on presidential bet to issue statement of support to people's mandamus! Million followers await you!

If VP Leni and all patriotic leaders will call democracy-loving Filipinos to sign the People Mandamus, we can collect millions of signatures. As of now we only have 18k!

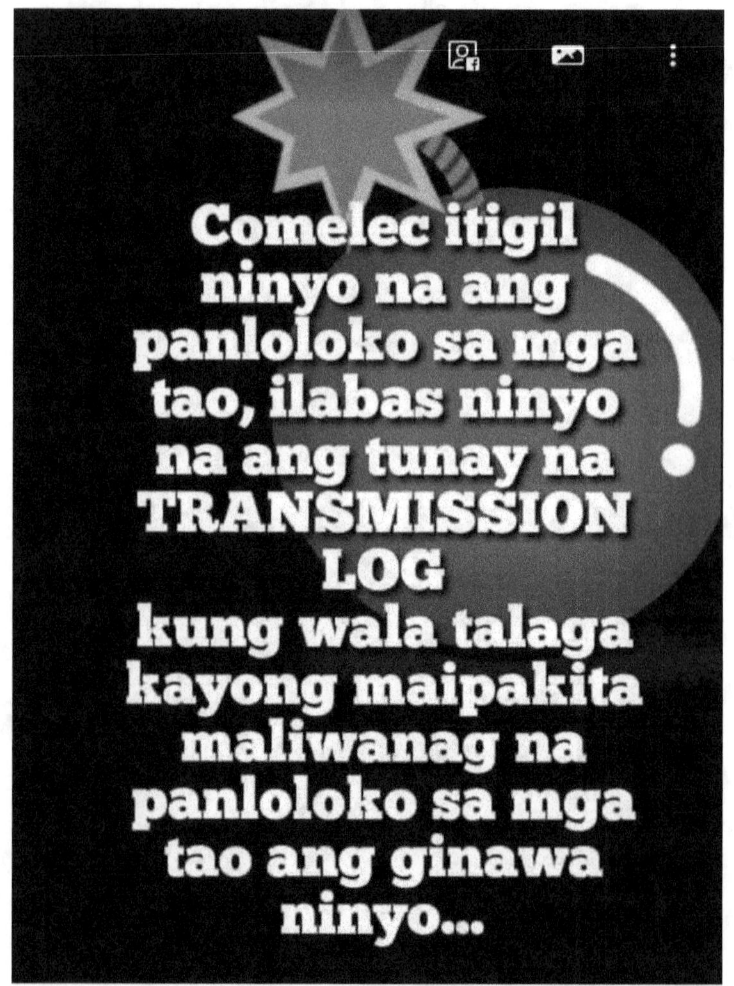

In science and in our political world, the key is " multiplier effect or value". As the saying goes,"you will reap what you sow"

Ano na, Opposition Leaders!

Ang Mandamus Petition sa Supreme Court ay tungkol sa karapatan ng mga mamayan na malaman ang katotohanan sa may patunay na pandaraya 'nung nakaraan na halalan. Dapat ipagtanggol ninyo ang nasabing karapatan.

We Deserve Better, Philippines

Ano na, Bayan?

How do you spell APATHY?

Apathy: F.I.V.E. M.O.R.E. Y.E.A.R.S
O.F. D.Y.N.A.S.T.I.C. R.U.L.E.
B.Y. T.H.E. U.N.I.T.H.I.E.V.E.S

Kilos na, Philippines

Ano na, Comelec!

HINDI KANAISNAIS AT
NAKAKASUKLAM ANG PATULOY
NA PAGTATAGO NG COMELEC NG
KATOTOHANAN TUNGKOL SA
PANDARAYA NUNG NAKARAAN
NA HALALAN. INAANTAY YATA
NA MAPUNO AT UMALSA ANG
BUONG BAYAN

We Deserve Better, Philippines

TAKE BACK OUR
DEMOCRACY!

Aimee F. Socorro B.
Ampoloquio Inting

George Marlon Rey E.
Garcia Casquejo Bulay

SUPPORT COL. ODONO'S
IMPEACHMENT MOVE
VS. THE COMELEC FOR
BETRAYAL OF THE
PUBLIC TRUST AND
CULPABLE VIOLATION
OF THE CONSTITUTION

I for one will not TOLERATE this. Let me put that on record. But if we as a people tolerate this blatant violation of our basic right of suffrage, then we deserve the government we get NOW AND IN THE FUTURE. We deserve the reputation that the world has given us.

We have to stop tolerating this! What we are ACTUALLY DOING is that because we lack the courage or concern to fight against these wrongdoings, we are simply passing the shame to the next generations for them to fix these themselves. And when they do, and surely they would, we will be remembered in history as the generation that tolerated injustice because we just thought of our personal interests and not of the National Interests.

- Gen. Eliseo Rio Jr.

Ano na, Opposition Leaders!

Ang pagsabi sa COMELEC na maglabas ng impormasyon na makakaayos sa matinding isyu ng dayaan sa nakaraang eleksyon ay walang gastos sa inyo. Umingay at makidamay!

Hindi Pera ang Isyu, Pilipinas

TNTrio are simply messengers of truth and true leaders are inspired to deliver the good from bad people!

A house built on lies will crumble on its own weight !

If VP Leni and all patriotic leaders will call democracy-loving Filipinos to sign the People Mandamus, we can collect millions of signatures. As of now we only have 18k!

A leader who lets the followers down is not a true leader during times of crisis !

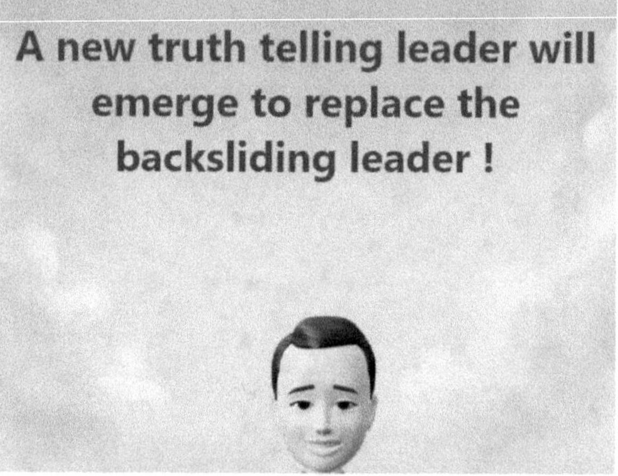

A new truth telling leader will emerge to replace the backsliding leader !

A true leader wakes up to the truth but the truth doesn't wait up for the true leader !

www.ingramcontent.com/pod-product-compliance
Lightning Source LLC
Chambersburg PA
CBHW051754250726

48659CB00001B/403